OPPOSITE CONTRARIES

OPPOSITE
CONTRARIES

THE UNKNOWN JOURNALS OF
EMILY CARR
AND OTHER WRITINGS

edited by Susan Crean

Douglas & McIntyre
VANCOUVER / TORONTO / BERKELEY

Douglas & McIntyre
2323 Quebec Street, Suite 201
Vancouver, British Columbia v5т 4s7
www.douglas-mcintyre.com

NATIONAL LIBRARY OF CANADA CATALOGUING IN PUBLICATION DATA

Carr, Emily, 1871–1945
Opposite contraries : the unknown journals of
Emily Carr and other writings / edited by Susan Crean.

Includes bibliographical references.
ISBN 1-55054-896-4

1. Carr, Emily, 1871–1945 — Diaries. 2. Painters — Canada — Biography.
I. Crean, Susan, 1945– II. Title.
ND249.C3A35 2003   759.11   C2003-910714-0

Editing by Saeko Usukawa
Design by Ingrid Paulson
Printed and bound in Canada by Friesens
Printed on acid-free paper

Distributed in the U.S. by Publishers Group West
Library of Congress Cataloging-in-Publication data is available

The publisher gratefully acknowledges the financial support of
the Canada Council for the Arts, the British Columbia Arts Council,
and the Government of Canada through the Book Publishing Industry
Development Program (BPIDP) for its publishing activities.

CONTENTS

Anyone who has gone looking for information in the public archives knows how seductive they are. How easily the material distracts attention from the task at hand, enticing you off on detours and down dead ends, one thing leading to another while the hours slip past in a stream. Like a trip to the Sally Ann, the search is often serendipitous: you go looking for one particular thing and come back with something else entirely, something you perhaps hadn't known you needed or even wanted. If the search is into a person's life, it is more like a treasure hunt. Lists aren't much help; intuition and visual alertness are your best assets, as chance and circumstance have more to do with what is left behind than rational activity on any person's part. Of course, the highly ordered conditions in which historical documents are kept — every page catalogued and accounted for — tend to contradict this. Nonetheless, "the record" is a capriciousness thing, and this is especially true of people who become famous late in life, as Emily Carr did. Lawren Harris, who met her in 1927 and corresponded with her over many years, but intensely through the period 1928–34 during her artistic flowering, did not keep her letters. A decade later, Ira Dilworth, who shepherded Carr's first book, *Klee Wyck*, into publication and watched the ailing painter receive a

Governor General's Literary Award for it in 1942, diligently kept her correspondence. For her part, Carr preserved the letters from both men. Harris had been an intellectual and artistic lifeline for her, a connection for which she was starved at the time. Dilworth, who was much more than an editor to her, inspired her confidences and her love, and his letters were longingly awaited and treasured. Writing to him in 1942, Carr mentions that she was rereading Harris's letters and had burned a few she thought too personal. Such was her attitude; she had kept Harris's letters for private reasons, but now she was keeping them for public ones. And, indeed, she was right. His letters to her serve as a unique record of the artistic crisis he underwent as he moved away from representational art into abstraction.

Archival research, I am suggesting, depends rather more on coincidence than people like to admit. And just as happenstance seems to control what makes its way into climate-controlled safekeeping, so the job of ferreting out the details that will tell the whole story years or decades later defies logic. It has as much or more to do with stamina and empathy than with intellectual application, for there is a psychological dimension to the activity; a spiritual relationship, you could almost say. Something like the bond that exists between birds and birders, which explains how it is you can sometimes go out into the woods and see nothing and at other times be astonished by the number and brilliance of the winged ones you encounter. In the archives, there are days when the slog over miles of curvilinear lettering strung across fields of yellowing paper yields nothing more than a sore neck and bleary eyes. And then there are moments when documents reveal themselves, as the birds do. It took time, but one day I realized I had finally got the gist of Carr's difficult handwriting and could read whole tracts of it without faltering. I had became familiar with her misspellings ("shure" for "sure") and contracted words, and could anticipate her meanings. I was no longer an intruder reading a script; I was present, listening to her speak. With birds, that same sort of thing happens when proximity between creature and human being becomes an unconscious thing, and the barrier in between disappears. It did the other night when a young barred owl, whose territory I inhabit on Gabriola Island, called to me from a perch in a fir tree high above the cabin porch. "Up here!" he insisted as I tried to find him in the twilight. Once spotted, he drifted down to a bare twig on the adjacent arbutus, closer, more visible, and curiously looked at me through great brown eyes. The ancients thought of owls as prescient and wise. Human beings have always warmed to their curiosity, their bold-ness and their throaty calls, but we are unnerved by their stealth and by the sense that they know something we do not. So it is with the business of wresting the past from piles of paper; the sense that truth lurks among them, if only we could see it.

Being familiar with archives, I was wary, reluctant to get involved. Yet, when Saeko Usukawa remarked to me one day that someone "really ought to go back and reread Emily Carr's actual journals," it started me thinking. Not being much of a betting person, the idea of rummaging through the forgotten corners of the Emily Carr archive on the lookout for missing bits of her story struck me as sentimental. How big could that archive be, anyway? How likely were any new revelations? As I had been researching Carr's life and afterlife as an icon to recent generations, I knew that the record was well worked over by biographers, art historians, artists, students, teachers, film-makers and the general public; and the list goes on.

Still, what was taken out of *Hundreds and Thousands*, the published journals, might indeed tell a story. Moreover, refer-ences in the literature to those expurgated sections, quotations from them and from some of the correspondence with Ira Dilworth, made me curious about the context in which they orig-inally had appeared. Already, one phrase from a letter that Carr wrote to Dilworth in November 1942 had become infamous: "the brutal telling" hangs like a cloud over Carr's story, giving rise to rumours of paternal abuse and sexual interference. So potent is it now that Vancouver choreographer Jennifer Mascall took the phrase as the title for the dance she created in 1998.

I set about planning an expedition to the British Columbia Archives in Victoria. The work would take several weeks and involve reading notebooks and letters written by hand and in pencil by Carr. I'd have to make a written transcript in pencil myself, as no pens are allowed. I'd need pencils, sharpeners, lined paper and a notebook to keep track of the project. I started off using the microfilm version of the journals, working in a dimly lit room reserved for the machines that display them, film on a grainy screen. By the end of the day, having had to stop twice in deference to the line of citizens waiting to do genealogical research and having then to find my place in the agonizing scrawl once again, my eyes were beyond tired; they felt awash with ground glass. Working on the horizontal and the vertical together, hopping from lighted screen to unlit page and back, transcribing the faded Carr text, was going to be impossible. I decided to appeal to the archivists on humanitarian grounds, and they graciously agreed to let me work with the originals. Wearing standard-issue white cotton gloves to protect the old paper from oily fingers and following a strict set of rules (sit where security can see you at all times, leave any and all food, drink, ink, pens, pocket knives and briefcases outside), I embarked.

My initial impression of the journals as I read them in the original was one of amazement. Despite Carr's struggles with writing and her conviction that she was deficient in both English grammar and stylistics, the prose in her journals is highly polished. Very little editing of any sort had been done to produce *Hundreds and Thousands: The Journals of Emily Carr*, which appeared posthumously in 1966 and has been in print ever since. As I began reading, I noticed that relatively little seemed to have been taken out. However, as I progressed through the scribblers, I found more outtakes and longer ones, approximately 45,000 words in all. In addition to passages and entries that formed part of the chronologically arranged and dated journals, there were several short stories or reminiscences, undated except by association with their place in the journals. These stories were each titled and seemed to be separate and unrelated except for the subject matter, the artist's life. They were started and restarted in several cases; most were scratched out whole as if they had been drafts.

The publisher's foreword to *Hundreds and Thousands* notes that Carr intended her journals to be published. While this is no doubt true, it is also evident from letters that the original idea for the book was a collection of stories in the format she had used for all her other books. It may be that she regarded her journals as raw material for that venture. Whatever the case, *Hundreds and Thousands* appeared twenty-one years after her

death, and four years after Ira Dilworth died. The journals were
not published as a literary memoir but as primary source material—the document as the writer left it. As such, and given
that they were written over the course of fifteen years and not
maintained as a regular practice, they are full of inconsistencies.
There are times, for instance, when Carr clearly is addressing
an audience, and other times when she is writing in breathless
point form to herself. You could swear she had forgotten anyone
was going to be reading them. Throughout, though, her voice
remains clear and sharp, and her own.

In addition to the original journals, the Emily Carr archive
contains her collected papers, correspondence and the manuscripts of her books. Among them, in typescript, is the short
autobiography that Carr wrote at the time she first went to eastern Canada in 1927 and also the text of a presentation she gave
about the Beacon Hill Galleries in 1932; this latter was her idea
for a public gallery in Victoria. Both documents are published
here for the first time. In longhand, and at much greater length,
is the "Lecture on Totems" that Carr delivered in 1913 on the
occasion of her first major exhibition in Vancouver. She had
rented the Dominion Hall on Pender Street, framed and hung
two hundred of her sketches and canvases, most of them dealing
with Native imagery, and invited the public to attend. Twice
during the week-long exhibit, she gave a public talk about the
paintings, explaining how they came to be made, how she had
travelled up the Skeena River and to the Queen Charlotte
Islands (Haida Gwaii) to record the carvings of a "disappearing"
and "primitive" people. Quoting the white experts of the day and
alluding to a Native informant, she gives a description of what

the images and totems were thought to signify in Native culture, what animals the various figures represented and so forth. Here, the seeds of *Klee Wyck* are planted; and, here, Carr recounts the story of her naming for the first time.

The "Lecture on Totems" is often mentioned and quoted in books about Carr. However, few people are aware that sections of *Klee Wyck* have been expurgated in the versions that followed the original Oxford University Press edition published in 1941. One whole story, "Martha's Joey," was removed, and several passages from two others, "Ucluelet" (about her first trip to a Native community in 1899) and "Friends"; as well, short bits from "Tanoo" and "Sophie" were deleted. "Martha's Joey" was restored in *The Complete Writings of Emily Carr* published by Douglas & McIntyre in 1993, and along with the deleted sections from the other stories is restored and republished here.

What else did my search uncover? The story of the feud between Emily and her niece, Una Boultbee. Details of the "brutal telling" and of Carr's unnamed first love. And evidence of her obsession with Bess Harris, and what Carr perceived as Bess's betrayal of their friendship. Carr had first known Bess Harris as Bess Housser, wife of the writer and theosophist Fred Housser. In 1934, the couple divorced, as did Lawren Harris and his wife, Trixie. Lawren and Bess subsequently married each other. Carr was one of the last to know about the "bust up," and she always felt that Bess had been dishonest in not telling her sooner.

The search also revealed a good deal about Sophie Frank, the First Nations woman whom Carr met in Vancouver in 1906, including information that shows her to be a literate person with much to contribute to Carr's artistic project as well as her emotional life. She could well be the "Squamish Indian" whom Carr mentions as a source in her "Lecture on Totems." And she is definitely the friend Carr commemorates when she dedicated *Klee Wyck* "To Sophie." The letters written by Sophie Frank (and the one from her husband, Jimmy Frank, to Carr, following Sophie's death in 1939), are the only documents in this volume not written by Carr. They are included because of their singular importance to the record and because, together with the heretofore unpublished passages about Sophie Frank in Carr's journals, they give substance to the friendship between the two women. One of the letters, written on August 6, 1915, has been published before, by Edythe Hembroff-Schleicher in *Emily Carr: The Untold Story* (page 102), but it is included here so that the small collection can been seen together.

And, finally, Emily Carr's correspondence with Ira Dilworth also adds to our knowledge about her emotional life, being a record of one of the few intimate friendships she sustained in her life. Like the relationship with Sophie Frank, this one, too, has largely gone unexamined by scholars. Only seven of the more than two hundred letters are printed here for reasons of space and because such a correspondence is best read with both sides of the exchange present.

Originally, I undertook the review of the Carr archive as research for a book I was writing on Carr and her legacy, called *The Laughing One: A Journey to Emily Carr*. Having benefited from the unpublished resource, and having appreciated the extent and particularity of it, I thought that more of it ought to be made accessible, that it should be put on the public record by way of being published as a book. Publisher Scott McIntyre agreed. The next step was locating the rights owner. Carr had left all her papers and manuscripts to Ira Dilworth, and these, in turn, had been passed down to his two adopted daughters, Phylis Inglis and Edna Parnall. All this material is now in the British Columbia Archives, but the Phylis Inglis collection almost did not make it. The federal government was approached when a bid was made by a wealthy Vancouver entrepreneur to buy the papers from Mrs. Inglis. The concern was that the Carr papers might be split up and that some of them might leave the country. Emergency funds were found and the collection was bought by the National Museums Corporation in 1976 and placed in the National Archives. In 1985 the Inglis collection was returned to British Columbia, to be housed in the provincial archives in Victoria. By 1999 none of these institutions knew exactly who owned the rights to the material. For though Carr died in 1945 and the normal term of copyright in Canada (life of the artist plus fifty years) was up, changes in the Copyright Act governing the publication of unpublished text material meant that the term covering the Inglis archive would not expire until 2004. The first step was to check the legacy through the chain of wills: Carr to Dilworth, Dilworth to Inglis and Parnall — and from there to whom? It took some sleuthing, but eventually I tracked down Phylis Inglis's son, the only progeny of the two sisters and the apparent owner of the rights in the unpublished material. He was elusive at first. Phone calls to members of the Parnall family produced shards of information but no offers of help; no one had seen him in years. Finally, I got an address and wrote directly, dreading silence or, worse, a flat rejection. Five days later the phone rang, and it was John Ira Dilworth Inglis, perfectly genial and willing to help. He reported that his mother had loathed Emily Carr and rid herself of all the paintings and memorabilia she had the moment that Ira Dilworth died in 1962. He himself had never investigated his inheritance or seen the archive, but he was happy to see it was still being used.

With Mr. Inglis's permission, a major portion of the Emily Carr archive now meets the light of day, notably the restored portions of the journals, Carr's earliest autobiographical statement and the text of her first public talk. This completes the personal record as Carr herself bequeathed it. Although caches of material (mostly correspondence) still remain to be unearthed from both public and private collections, this publication, together with Carr's already published books, represents the voice of the artist narrating her own life. That voice spans thirty-two years of her career in this volume, from her public debut as an independent artist in 1913 to the last weeks of her life in 1945.

The title of this volume comes from Emily Carr's journals. It appears in a passage in which Carr describes a journey by train from Chicago back to Canada in 1933. "Life is full of opposite contraries," she declares as she watches the countryside slipping by through the window, noticing turkeys roosting on barn rooftops, away from the icicles. "Opposite contraries" was indeed the way Carr viewed the world. As the journals attest, she was endlessly fascinated by differences between people and between places. Even as a child, she was attuned to the hypocrisy imbedded in the transplanted English culture of her father's generation, and in reaction she embraced the West and its people for what it was and what they had become. She started early down the path of difference, becoming a contrary within her family, and then remaining a contrary within Canadian society all her life. Emily Carr was a woman who consciously did things differently, and even though this difference bedevilled her, she embraced it.

Susan Crean
Gabriola Island

PART ONE

Previous page: Emily Carr and her brother Dick in 1891. B.C. Archives I-60892

The cxpurgated portions of the journals of Emily Carr fall into two categories: one comprises passages, sometimes entire entries, left out of *Hundreds and Thousands*, and the other comprises a handful of short stories that are in the notebooks in which Carr kept her journals but are plainly not part of them.

What was edited out of *Hundreds and Thousands* is indicative. The story of Carr's break with her older sister Clara's daughter, Una Boultbee, which featured a silence of eleven or twelve years, set off by a letter that Emily saw and wasn't supposed to, involved people who were still living in 1966 when the journals were first published. Decorum and libel laws may have suggested this be cut. To avoid repetition, a good many passages detailing angst about her family were also left out, along with several of the searing laments over her (thus far) fruitless artistic quest, a quest she viewed, more and more, as a spiritual one. The work of preparing *Hundreds and Thousands* for publication was begun by Ira Dilworth and, after he died, was completed by the publishers with the help of Phyllis Inglis. Collectively, these editors took a dim view of Carr's gratuitous commentary, particularly her scathing remarks about people's looks and behaviour, observed while she was attending social events or travelling about (Carr's trip to Chicago by train in 1933 is the main example of this). These were unceremoniously dropped from the published version. Similarly, the diatribes against her tenants seemed excessive and were trimmed. Passages of both types are included here in some number, but not in their entirety for the same reasons of excess and repetition.

The unpublished portions of the journals also contain the inside view of Carr's spiritual return to Christianity, her struggle with theosophy having resulted in its rejection, and the initiation of a new search outside the main circle of the established Christian church and received Protestant wisdom. Here are long philosophic ruminations about the sermons of the men whom she sought out as spiritual guides: Raja Singh, Garland Anderson and Clem Davies. Almost as long but more frequent are the passages, better described as laments, about her sisters and their inability to cherish her, about her poor fit in the Carr family. These are included, too, but not exhaustively, as Carr indulged in tedious repetition on this subject — another indication that the journals were not always meant for readers and at least sometimes provided a place where she tussled with demons.

The removed sections contain some spicy commentary on the sexual politics of her day: on the fickleness of female friendship, for instance; of the disdain of married women for spinsters, and of the general untrustworthiness of men. She writes about the profundity of motherhood and, by comparison, the puny purpose of fatherhood. Observing the way these roles play out in human and animal families, she speaks of sex and her preference for the uncluttered approach of animals and her distaste for the overheated, low and dirty attitude of people. She discusses her own aversion to sex, citing horror stories and tragedies, but also, occasionally, mentions some poignant exceptions she has observed. She expresses her conclusion that marriage is at best a mutual convenience and at worst a sham.

All of the short stories within the journal notebooks are titled, and some are easily recognizable as drafts for sections that appear in *Klee Wyck*, *The Book of Small* and *Growing Pains*, the latter written in the last few years of her life and published posthumously. (Carr actually compiled the manuscript of *Growing Pains* in book form, complete with a handmade cover, as a present to Ira Dilworth for Christmas in 1941.) The story "Martyn" in *Growing Pains* is about a young man who loved the young Emily and pursued her to England, hoping she would relent in her decision against marrying him. There are three drafts of this, but as they are all close cousins of the published version, they are not included here. Another short piece, a discarded version of the opening to the story "Sophie" that appears in *Klee Wyck*, details the first meeting of Carr and Sophie Frank in Carr's studio in Vancouver, around 1906. Two stories of Carr's childhood, "British Columbia Nightingales" and "Young Town and Little Girl" are likewise early and quite different versions of "British Columbia Nightingales" and "Saloons and Roadhouses" in *The Book of Small*. The first recounts her father's joke about the sound of tree frogs mating in the spring, and the second is about Richard Carr's store, downtown by the docks. In both cases, the changes involved taking out sections describing racial difference. In the first instance, details of the dress and manner of Bong, the Carr family's Chinese manservant, are deleted; in the second, vocabulary is altered. The three other stories— "Mother," "Love" and "A Dream"— have never been published in any form in Carr's books, though there is another story entitled "Mother" in *Growing Pains*.

Perhaps what is most noticeable in reading the journal "outtakes" is the host of racial slurs, starting with Carr's entries about "the Jew" who lived next door to her on Beckley Street, and her references to black people as "niggers." She describes "niggertown" in Chicago, for instance, and is prompted to wonder out loud, "I can see the American Indian falling in step with the white races and the Eastern peoples — Chinese and Japanese — but I can't see the niggers. I like them but I don't feel sisterly exactly." In "Young Town and Little Girl," she tells the story of being snatched out of harm's way by a black man when some cattle stampeded down Wharf Street in front of her father's store. He whisks her into a saloon and plops her onto the bar where she sits agog, torn between wanting to watch the wild animals carrying on outside and wanting to take in her first sight of the inside of a drinking establishment. The version of the story published in 1942 avoids the word "nigger" entirely (referring to the man as either a "black man" or "Negro") and reworks the ending, changing the focus of the story from its emphasis on race to one highlighting the social disgrace represented by bars and saloons.

At the same time, other expurgated sections of the journal indicate that Carr was not at all ignorant of race issues. She notes that people reacted more superficially to her paintings of Native imagery than to her newer landscape sketches, and implies it is because the creation was not all hers. And in a passage about a Mr. Shades who was obsessed with Native artifacts, whose "soul rolls around Indian designs, colours, robes" and who had "done his summer house up Indian," Carr writes: "There is a falseness about a white man using those symbols to ornament himself. The Indian believed in them. They expressed him. The white is not expressing himself; he's faking." It would seem that Carr was quite conscious of the racism around her and was not reticent about chastizing white society for its intolerance and superior attitudes. However, she was not able to turn the critique on herself, tending instead to promote herself as the exception, a special friend and interlocutor for Native culture. She is conflicted and inconsistent. In discussing her friendship with Sophie Frank, Carr is doubly enigmatic, telling us very little about her beyond the usual stereotypes; Carr praises her lavishly and folds Sophie Frank's character and story into her literary project while actually disguising the friendship and misrepresenting the real person to posterity.

Nowhere is ambivalence in Carr more evident than in her handling of the subject of love. She is coy, suggestive and, in the end, deliberately (one suspects) gives us clues but not the whole story. On combing the journal manuscript, for example, while I did find the occasional phrase and clause deleted, none of them were of any moment except for one. In the published entry for January 9, 1938, the second-last line is missing six words. The passage begins with the reflection that her love had endured three crushing blows in life. This is followed by a sentence of six words that was twelve in the original:

> *I have loved three souls, passionately,* passionately, two relatives and a lover.

Her father, obviously, was one of the two relatives, and the nature of her relationship with him is explored in several entries as well as in a letter to Ira Dilworth. But the other relative remains a complete mystery. Carr rarely mentions her brother Dick, who died in a tuberculosis sanatorium in California in 1899 shortly after she arrived in England (the news came with her first letter from home). A set of studio photographs dating from 1891 shows the brother and sister together. In one, they appear in a formal pose and street attire, but in the other, they are in a relaxed pose of easy and intimate affection. The gloves and hat are gone, and Carr stands behind her younger brother, who is seated, leaning into him, arms crossed and resting on his shoulder. This photo is impossibly little to go on, of course, and the very idea might seem to imply incestuous feelings on her part, though perhaps not. The expurgated journals and other writings in this volume indicate that her conflict with her father was not obviously the result of sexual abuse; they demonstrate that the conflict between them had an intellectual and emotional content that does not presuppose incest any more than it precludes it. Is it possible that Carr had a special relation with her brother that ended when he died and that his death was one of the blows to which she refers? She wrote, albeit briefly, about Clara, her oldest sister, who married and left home before Carr was a teenager, so it does seem odd that she scarcely mentions Dick. He is the blue-eyed, curly blond little brother with whom she had to have been close, physically if nothing else, because of their proximity at the end of a long line of children, with only three years separating them. She wrote about her father, her mother, the hired help and endlessly about her sisters, so why, then, if there was special love and hurt between herself and Dick, did she never write about him? Yet there are no other candidates. She could be referring to her mother or even possibly one of her sisters, though all are improbable, specifically because she wrote so much about them, otherwise. So, in the end, the identities of the two passionately beloved "relatives" are left to our imagination and conjecture, perhaps deliberately.

With the vignette called "Love" (heavily scratched out in the original), wherein Carr recounts her traumatic first encounter with romance and sex, together with the other excised entries referring to her Manichaean tussle with love, we are now in a position to know something about the person she is referring to when she mentions the lover. Not enough to suggest the young man's identity, but enough to place him in her biography and to illuminate the allusion to "love found" in *Hundreds and Thousands*. That Carr clearly wanted the story known but was not willing to revive the humiliation by divulging names is evident in her obvious delight in telling half the story, in her candour coated with ambiguity.

A good deal has been written on the subject of Carr's relationship with her father, Richard Carr, particularly his crude introduction to the facts of life and its seismic aftermath. References to this event in letters to Ira Dilworth, together with the short piece entitled "Mother" and the journal description (April 22, 1935) of Carr's reflections when she and her two elderly sisters reread their father's diaries, offer a rather more positive view of the man than he has had heretofore. Similarly, the consternation, the dreams and the caustic comments about Bess Harris that pop up throughout the journals indicate an emotional tie of significant proportions between Bess and Emily that has not been evident before. They reveal an anger that lasted long enough for the disaffection to become common knowledge, it being widely known in art circles that Emily Carr had no use for Bess Harris. The other side of the story is the depth of feeling involved, the love that preceded the bitterness.

The second person who haunts Carr's subconscious during these years is Sophie Frank. Carr writes of Sophie with unrestrained love and refers repeatedly to their spiritual connection and mutual trust, to the special quality of their love. She also tells tales about Sophie's drunkenness, her reputed stint on the streets and her fall from grace (in Carr's eyes), so it would appear that there was a rupture in this friendship too. Carr does not hide her judgementalism. Sophie's behaviour was abhorrent to her and violated all sense of decency as she understood it. Yet her desire to think well of Sophie, to think of their love as unconditional, triumphed. One wonders, though, how this might have felt to Sophie; whether or not she forgave Emily the same way, whether or not she took the white woman to heart in return.

The previously unpublished portions of Carr's journals are presented here in chronological order and are grouped under the same headings as in *Hundreds and Thousands*. As with *Hundreds and Thousands*, the restored excerpts peter out in the last years — 1939, 1940 and 1941 — as Carr became increasing ill and unable to write. Some of the restored excerpts, for the sake of comprehension, have required presentation in context, which is to say within the published passage from which they were deleted; the previously published fragments are italicized. Furthermore, an ellipsis within italicized square brackets *[...]* marks the beginning of an entry that follows a published section, or the end of an entry that precedes a published section, or an omission within a published section; an ellipsis within roman square brackets [...] marks an omission in an unpublished section. Words added for understanding or not readable in the original manuscript are in square brackets.

Carr's text is reproduced here as it was written; her syntax is not altered, though her spelling is regularized, some punctuation is introduced and some excessive underlining removed. (Her underlinings are indicated here by italics.) As a rule, she preferred to write without capital letters at the beginning of sentences and with commas in lieu of periods. This often gives her prose the feel of stream-of-consciousness writing, and occasionally this takes off like a riff on a tenor saxophone. Although she often writes in short snappy sentences, more often they are long and convoluted, and though confusing without the presence of commas and colons, they usually do scan for sense. In this way, Emily Carr has to be appreciated as an accomplished prose stylist very much in control of the language.

Carr had a title for her journals, which she inscribed on the inside cover page of the lined notebook she began in November 1930. "Oddments on Thoughts and Feelings on Work," she called them, and so they emerged, patchwork, piecework: part story, part reflection, part confession.

SIMCOE STREET
1930–33

AUGUST 19TH, 1930

[Emily Carr's final trip to Native sites on northern Vancouver Island, with her dog Koko]

Left home midnight of August 19 for Alert Bay sketch trip, taking Koko. Phil saw me off. We sat on bags and had ginger ale and a cigarette on the wharf. Long nights.

Vancouver, 7 A.M.

Rather misty or smoky. The recent CNR fire must have been frightful. The charred remains were pitiful. I went right over to North Vancouver to see Sophie. My heart stood still when I found the gate nailed up, the house forsaken. I thought she might be dead, but the Indian next door, who came at my rap half-naked, told me she was away with Frank hops picking. I went to see the church and prayed earnestly for help with my work and for Sophie. It is very quiet and lovely and peaceful in the little Catholic church in the early morning. One forgets the tawdriness. The Virgin looks so serene and St. Joseph so kindly and there is the Christ Child and the crucified Christ. The altar was decked with flowers. Some were *real* from Indian gardens — astis and perennial phlox purple pink. I went up rickety stairs into the gallery. There were signs of many rats. It was ill kept and littered cobwebs hung. There were rat holes in odd corners. So I went below again and sat quiet with my arm around Koko. Then I went on past the derelict boats lying in the mud and the derelict houses leaning, broken dreary windows stuffed with rags; derelict cats scuttled off under houses across the accumulated litter of rubbish, between the drunken foundation blocks of drift[wood] that the houses are set upon. Quite a portentous house is being built on the church green. Will it have as good an ending as beginning? They always tire and leave their buildings half-complete.

Sara was well locked and barred as to gate. Her big perennial phlox was blooming lavishly, its circumference circled with rags to help it from being wind wrecked. The steps and narrow railless verandah were more dilapidated than ever. Boards tipped as you trod. I stepped warily and it took Sara some wrestling with the key and some jiggling to get it [the door] open. There she stood in a very clean undervest and meagre shawl, also clean, and a cotton skirt gathered fully into belts that would not meet and had no fastenings. The wrinkles of her face did wonderful gymnastics around their "It's Emily!" There was no doubting her welcome. "Lumatism bad. Here and here." She pulled up garments and down garments to show me the misshapen members and crawled back to her bed, a veritable mountain of patchwork quilts and oddments with white pillows and sheets, an eructation of woollies built in stacks and covered with every manner of rag to help keep off draughts. With a long stick she hooked about her, gathering a blouse made of several different pattern prints, a few more cotton skirts and a pin cushion stick with scissors, and as she talked she pinned things about her. Her thick iron-grey hair hung in a heavy plait. She is life weary and full of pains. We'd a great talk and then we spoke of Sophie. The news is bad. Sophie is drinking and worse. Though she is Sophie's aunt she has nothing to do with her now. I wondered how much was true. I went on to the priest's house, a worn green thing next to the church, little better than the Indians'. He ambled down the stairs at my knock. I had never talked with him before. A dirty little man who lisps a lot but not pleasantly. He confirmed all. Sophie is a prostitute. She is drinking hard. She is always over in town. A woman on the street, the chattel of the lowest waterfront derelicts. Frank takes her to them and waits while she earns the beastly dollar. Then they drink. Poor Sophie who I have loved so. She has lied hideously and sunk so low and there is little one can do. She's the worst in the village and leading all the young girls wrong too. She used to be good and straight and true yet she's had so much trouble. Twenty-one children all dead and she loved them so every one. Sophie that told me that she loved me like a sister, and that I loved and believed.

Quatsino

It is early Sunday morning. I came last night, slithering through the still waters of Quatsino Sound on the flat little mail boat bulging all over with mailbags and stuff. I sat on the back deck on a big mail sack with my back to a barrel. Koko in my arms, the two of us covered with my oilskin coat. The great September moon was playing hide-and-seek, an overgrown baby way behind the clouds; and then it moved back behind mountains and tall trees, leaving us in the dark. It loved to tantalize, hiding away just as one felt that we were getting to a particularly lovely bit. Then I sat in the dark and wondered things. Life has always been like that—wondering why. I remember lying on my bed in the little north bedroom and fancying that all over the low ceiling where the roof sloped was written great "whys." Well, I wondered about all the mail I sat among, who would get these letters, what they'd say and feel, and how the letters would give them joy or sorrow or perplexity, or tell of births and deaths and marriages. It seemed as if I could feel portentous things in men's and women's lives poking out of the sacks. Letters that had been longed for and letters that had been dreaded and unexpected letters that would be too late. Then the engine made queer noises and I wondered if things were OK below. The engineer had been on the stage from Hardy Bay. We had had to wait for him at the beer parlour, he and another man, and they walked foolishly, were both obviously a little drunk. When I knew one was our engineer I felt indignant that brutes like that had human lives at their mercy. They're not fit to have charge even of "His Majesty's mail." There were, I think, only a couple of passengers besides myself. A gentleman (how they tell out in this country of slouch and rude speech) and a China-man. Except for the clang there was absolute silence. No one spoke. Perhaps they were wondering too—wondering why an old woman, very shabby and uncommunicative, was sitting there on the mail sacks, hugging a wee dog. Eventually there were lights and a series of bumps and heavy uncouth forms around barrels and boxes. No women. I clambered over the side and then asked where the hotel was and where I paid my boat fare. After a bit a man came from somewhere and took my dollar and a slouching old man took my bags. We went over long uneven board floats with gaping holes and unevenness, up a steep little bank and through a cow gate. A few giggling girls and loutish boys stood around the pot of fire at the store waiting for the mail to be sorted. They stared rudely at me. The hotel keeper was plump and kindly. She showed me to a room on the ground floor. The beds were clean and at first sight I thought it looked not bad. But daylight reveals much dirt, cigarette stubs, dead flowers, matches and, loathsome to a degree, someone has been drunk sick behind the bureau. These whites are little better than the Indians in clean habits. Koko and I walked behind the house a bit. It was very still and lovely. Koko was tired and fixed his head on my coat behind my red canvas bag and snored grumpily. I had a splitting headache, the rough churning on the sea earlier in the day and the tiresome wait at Hardy Bay had frayed my nerves and temper and brought on a splitter. But I had an aspirin and read one of the three books provided in my room, A *Vindication of the Life of Lady Byron.* I slept and I dreamed.

What do these forests make you feel? Their weight and density, their crowded orderliness. There is scarcely room for another tree and yet there is space around each. They are profoundly solemn yet upliftingly joyous; like the Bible, you can find strength in them that you look for. How absolutely full of truth they are, how full of reality. The juice and essence of life are in them; they teem with life, growth and expansion. They are a refuge for myriads of living things. As the breezes blow among them, they quiver, yet how still they stand developing with the universe. God is among them. He has breathed with them the breath of life, might and patience. They stand developing, springing from tiny seeds, pushing close to Mother Earth. Fluffy baby things first, sheltering beneath their parents, mounting higher, spreading brave branches, pushing with mighty strength not to be denied, skywards. Tossing in the breezes, glowing in the sunshine, bathing in the showers, bending below the snow piled on their branches, drinking the dew, rejoicing in creation, bracing each other, sheltering the birds and beasts, the myriad insects.

Cat Village

Above the dip of oars came the meows, the prolonged beseeching. There was not a soul in the village. Every Indian was away fishing, had been for months, the little gas boats had gone. The carriers first take the women and the children, the dogs and cats, but not all, evidently. The boat hull grated. Gumbooted and carrying Koko, I clambered over the side. Three cats waited for me on the pebbly beach. Ugly mottled lean yellow-eyed beasts. The man and boat left. Another cat joined me, and a speckled poulet. They crowded around my feet just wanting sympathy, kind words, companionship. Sure as they knew water was wet they knew Koko and I could be trusted. They crowded round my feet, purring and rubbing, meowing. Their yellow eyes gleaming, tails erect, ears erect; every step I took, they took. They crowded round my camp stool, quarrelling who should get next me after the first wary look to see how I took it. Koko slept with one eye shut, guarding me with the other. The cats purred and rubbed, and the poulet chortled confidently and lay on her side with one yellow leg stretched out and her feathers loosened for the sun to reach her skin.

I worked all day. When I ate, the cats and the poulet shared my bread and cheese. When I moved about the village, they followed in meowing procession. At night I left them meowing dolefully at the very edge of the sea.

Next day I went again. Before the engine had stopped, before I was in the scow boat, I heard them. Not four but eight running the water's edge and meowing like the Hallelujah Chorus. One had jumped into the boat before I landed. There were the speckled four and the surprisingly white ones, a tortoiseshell, some kittens, a battered half-Persian. The purring sounded like a beehive. Yellow eyes were all agleam. I could scarcely walk without treading on them. They meowed and rubbed ten times harder than yesterday. We climbed the rotten driftwood stair up the bank. My courtiers and I halfway were met by the splendid poulet. She came running and followed by a clucking hen. She clucked from habit, nothing responding. Probably her brood had found homes in the cats' stomachs. From 9 to 6 I worked and my court surrounded me. They tried to swarm into my lap and upon my shoulders. This I could not permit. Indian cats are filthy cats, carry things. They were like a lot of children quarrelling who should sit next to teacher.

I went back into the woods. The undergrowth was dense but there were fresh deer tracks and paths broken by deer and probably panther and bear. It was creepy, but my cats all came through too, the speckleds and the tabby, the tortoiseshell and the whites. All day long they stayed with me, pressing close and closer; when the boat came, the whole procession came to the water. I thought one was going to swim out. She jumped on a log out in the sea, then jumped back and followed along the beach. One did board the boat. The Persian. Perhaps she felt herself more out of place than the rest. I hated to leave them to their loneliness.

It was a queer experience. I've never had one feeling quite like it. Indian cats are usually mean, timid, slinky creatures, scurrying out of the way of the children who abuse them and the dogs who hound them. They have little use for humans. What did the cats know about me? Why such absolute trust and affection and understanding? I talked to them. Poor beasties, your "Mom" knows, I said. Same as I tell Koko.

I shall always remember those cats, my cat party, the feeling of perfect understanding between us all. Life is all one. The unexplainable spark that touches us all binds us all. Life. LIFE.

Waiting

Most three quarters of life up here is waiting. Waiting for boats, waiting for stages, waiting for mail, waiting for meals. While this country waits for development and the race awaits evolving. All the foreign elements incorporated into the white, the white elements incorporated into the foreign. The Indian watches his race disappear yet not disappear; appearing in a new civilization, new manners, new customs, new looks, yet with a trifle in them of himself. The new race gathering, sifting, sorting. The hillsides wait 'til the loggers come; strange upheavals, strange noises, vibrations, swells, burning, cutting, blasting. Out of it all springs the second growth, springing joyous, buoyant, new, new; yet it could not have existed except for the old. The sea remains as of old but everywhere boats toss and puff and snort, her silver [waters] are [keeping] the ships clean and they pollute her with offal. But she is vast, vast. The sky? Yes, they are catching her sounds and secrets; they intake her with the aeroplanes. Spaces are linked we are getting to know.

S.S. Card[ena] *Southbound, September 11–19, 1930*

It is good to be going home. There's the girls and the monk and the cat and the tenants and the flowers, even if one dreads the survey business. In whining, of course, things'll get the better of me, being a woman.

It's grey but luminous. I breakfasted opposite a drunk which disgusted me so I made a very scant meal. I was afraid he'd be sick. The dried-up dame next him seemed oblivious. She [chewed] as calmly as a cow and ordered everything. She had coarse straight hair, half long and hanging, a yellow skin, glasses, and a red and black garment that looked like a uniform and wasn't. I should say she was a missionary connection.

Men are doing the parade. First, they started singly, now most have doubled up, the very tall ones, the short, an uneven pair. A bullescent mother with a bored son. They are both in sweaters (new for the voyage), her skirt is very much riding up and her legs look old. She waddles. A big Swede is washing paint. He does every part about five times. I can't make out if he's being thorough or very careless. The men all look so fleshy, so very material, as though what minds they had were full of dinner and money.

I have not seen my roommate yet. She did make me furious, bursting into the stateroom about midnight and tearing aside my curtains and staring at me. I ripped them back on the rod violently. Neither of us said a word. She read a telegram that had just come for her and went out and banged the door. It was well on with morning before she came to bed. I got up early and left her sleeping.

MONDAY, NOVEMBER 24TH [1930]
This morning I've tried the thing on canvas. It's poor. I got a letter from [Mark] Tobey today. Oh, the creature, he is so spineless. His letter was all tales of excuse for his tardiness in not acknowledging my letter and money. (I sent him the fare to come over 3 weeks ago to give me a crit.) He wanted to come and I know he was short. Well, sadly, $5 and no crit. I sent back a brief note: "No use coming now. Pictures are all away and I expect a guest and won't have room for you." Poor worm. Clever and so sorry for himself because he has to make a living. If he'd only get busy. Everything he does is with money first in his brain and it kills his work. *He is clever but his work has no soul. It's clever and beautiful. [...]*

SUNDAY, JANUARY 11TH, 1931

No word from Hatch about the Seattle show. I don't feel it has been a success at all. Hatch said it had made a stir. No one went away without saying something. Some good, Some bad. *At least it waked them up. That's something. [...]*

WEDNESDAY, JANUARY 28TH

[...] I wrote two letters, one to Mr. Fuller, president of the Seattle Art Institute. I asked him to find out what was happening about my pictures. Hatch did not answer, I said. Just as I finished it, I got a line from Hatch. It was useless to try and find things that way. Ignoring all my questions. Nothing decided yet. He'd been away in the South "playing around." It's rot; the man's a slacking fool. I wrote him a scorcher, typed every word and may do him good. It'll settle my head. My things will come bobbing home to the sound of a loud Amen! But I don't care. I feel lots better for exploding. The sun began to shine at once and now I'm off to the woods to rejoice. I wonder if Fuller will show him my letter. It was written in "fist" so pr'aps he can't read same. Don't care anyhow — why not be decent and honest in art business as any other? They ought to be *better* and *higher* and *principled* because art should create all the best in us in every way. Slacking and dallying is not best. It's dishonourable and belittling.

JANUARY 29TH

Mrs. Pinkerton thinks I did wrong in sending Hatch that outburst. I'd have come to an untimely end if I had bottled [it] up any longer. Of course he'll be quit of me now, like Ottawa, having all their own way. They think they are so noble, shoving you forward into the beastly public eye — that and being "written up." And these ideas of an artist's ambitions, hopes and desires, that's the idea of Mrs. Pinkerton too. She thinks one should swallow anything just to get before the public. Oh, oh, oh, oh, oh. No! That spoils everything; even unconsciously it leads to smugness, draws away from concentration from striving for the great things.

JANUARY 31ST

Today I am a bundle of nerves. Reaction, probably, from the storm within over Hatch's letter and feeling like a swine. Was I unfair to him? After all, why should he bother with my rotten stuff at all? Damn. I'm always like that, bursting forth making enemies instead of friends, whirling around in a muck of rage, muddling everything and getting all wrought up. How can [I] see straight and clear and search for the good, the true and the beautiful when I'm such a wild beast—and yet I go on just swallowing everything, seeing things going wrong and rotten. Then I ferment inside and that's worse. One must be calm and happy according to one of my teachers, a Frenchman who used to badger me to get the best work out [of me], he said. Maybe it was more alive work, but this is not what one wants. It is deep, pure, good. Good emotion that should underlie the best work—not mean snappy ones.

I shall never paint anything good. I am just dead bones and venom, and I ache to express what is really good and beautiful and true and real.

WEDNESDAY, FEBRUARY, 4TH

Lizzie, Alice and I went to hear the Seattle Symphony. [...] Good music that gives one the best feelings always leads me away from man, away from cities out and off to spaces (or woods). Why? Being human, the call of humanhood should be stronger. *[...]*

SUNDAY, FEBRUARY 22ND
[...] How weary I am of showing off my pictures. Seattle people who have anthropologists' interest in my old Indian stuff. The man deaf and the woman stupid. Well, it gave me an opportunity to clean behind the picture anyway. . . .

Look up and feel out to every corner of the earth. Loving people and things and searching after God — and after the good and true and the beautiful.

APRIL 17TH
[...] Just come from the fourth lecture in a course on applied psychology with Harry Gage. Have enjoyed them enormously — practical, straightforward, inspiring. Last night's lecture was more spiritual and wonderful. He taught on the "silence," on meditation and concentration. The silence is turning one's mind to the infinite divine, absolute communion with the divine. Telepathy is conveying by your subconscious to the other fellow's subconscious (since time and space do not count). Tonight was [on] food. He recommends no meat or fish or sparingly. Lots of salad, vegetables, some root vegetables. Never more than one starch and abundance of fruit, nuts. Some milk and eggs. No tea or coffee. Water and fruit juice for drinks.

JULY 14TH
[Lizzie Carr was called Betty by most people]
Just home from a psychology lecture by Professor Mobius. Funny duck, but I got quite a bit out of it. Then came home and

straightway forgot B.C. [Betty Carr]. Why does she rile me so? Her religion, which she thrusts at one every occasion, is so small and mean. Somehow her God seems such a small little person.

I wouldn't give a bean to Gardner's wedding present. I [have] died to that outfit. When Una said she hoped sincerely I'd die and not live to be a cranky invalid [for] poor Lizzie to care for, I did die to her. When I read that, Lizzie says I'm wicked, she always has and always will side with any other human being on earth against me. That's been her attitude towards me and my things and my painting and all pertaining to me always. And she always throws a sneaky religious cloak over her statements. I don't like her religion and I don't want it. I don't believe God is small and mean and unjust as she paints him.

JANUARY 25TH, 1933

I've been figuring out with myself how it is I hate write-ups. Someone always sticks them under my nose. I figure thus: people here don't like my work, it says nothing to them, but they like what is said about it in the East. In other words, they like the "kick up" not it. That's the hurt. I'd rather have a nigger or an idiot really like the work itself (feel something in it) than the governor general gloat over a spiel on it. [...]

SEATON LAKE, PSE

[Trip in June 1933 to Pemberton, British Columbia, written on separate sheets]

As I knelt in the little Catholic church this came to me — crude pictures of Christ and the Virgin and St. Joseph, as the church was too little and poor to buy statues. Such a few moneyless Indians left in the village, such a full graveyard. The bare floor — no benches or pews — the wooden altar built crooked and off-plumb by the Indians and smeared over with only one coat of paint — whitish leaning to pink and green as though odd bits of paint had been put together to make enough. The cheap coloured glass in the four tiny narrow pointed windows — one green, one red, one blue, one yellow. Six candles, three each side of the cheap crucifix. Some withered lilacs in tin cans and marmalade pots, and a few cheap artificial flowers. Above the altar, three pictures of Christ in homely wood frames, crudely fashioned with a cross cut in the top of each. Christ on the cross, Christ with the crown of thorns, Christ with the flaming heart of love. In the corner Christ again, one hand upraised in blessing, the other pointing to his heart, a wreath of thorns around it, blood drops falling. In the opposite corner, Mary and around her heart a wreath of roses. No sound but a mother hen outside calling her chicks and the chortle of blackbirds getting food for their young. Great peace. What was there, I asked, in the crude pictures on the wall that inspired your reverence? That lifted your spirit and satisfied surely? They were very crude, not works of art as the world counts art. And the answer came, no, "but works of spirit." The makers of these originals had sought to portray not man or woman, but to find symbols for love, purity, holiness. With their minds on these things, something had happened — something had come into expression — something that spoke in wordless words to the soul. So, I said to myself, must I seek spiritual symbols, attributes of God in this that I would paint? See God in his creation, become conscious of the Maker in His universe without searching or struggling but being still and open to receive illumination with my mind always upon God, seeing in His manifestation symbols of the Creator.

I am groping horribly lost, trying to search for that thing. It is right here and yet I do not know how to find it, it is in me and yet so far away I cannot reach it. I don't know where to look and I want it so badly I'm sick — yet I'm dumb and bound — if I only knew what binds me so I could tear it off. If my eyes were only not blind so I could see, and my numb senses so quiveringly alert and sensitive that I could feel in every fibre of me the ecstasy of comprehension. Oh you old fool. Come down. Clear out your heart and mind and soul. Fast and pray — the body material predominates so — I am a slave to the flesh, and the spirit strays and gasps — it cannot soar because it is weighted down by fleshy things. Good food, comfort, laziness, bodily ailments. Cannot the spirit dominate the liver? Throw out the depression, rise above inertia? I am a slacker.

What is it Ziegler said? "Do not try to *force* those great forests, woo them." It is I [who] must seek first the true spirit of humble worship, the spirit of communion with the infinite, the allness of God in the universe. Perhaps it is *this* one must seek to find in others. I feel things clearer when I am away from humans in the woods. God seems there more — why? To be sure he is out there among the silent things but not among his highest life creations — man. One should feel him more when amongst those creatures made in his image and likeness — why is it we don't? Man has answered God back, being saucy and irreverent. Dumb nature has obeyed, goes ahead according the seasons — lives silently — is the mystery of things and sings everlasting praise to the eternal.

In B.C., epochs ago, was a narrow lake three to six miles long, and on each side stood great, austere mountains frowning down upon its clear surface. Then came some gigantic upheaval and one of the biggest mountains toppled and sat down plumb in the middle of the lake and filled [it] up so that it was doubled into two lakes, each 18 miles long. The southern is called Anderson Lake and the other one, Seaton. For a long time water slapped the sitting-down mountain, but after years the water made a bed for itself and the mountain that was dried out, and made rich land. Farms were planted here and the bare broken side of the mountain, which was worn and scarred, healed up, and a great forest of young pines covered it.

THE ELEPHANT
1933

AUGUST 31ST

A wet day in camp. The rain pattered on the top of the Elephant all night. Mrs "Pop Shop" and I went for our nightly dip in the river. It was cold and took courage and much squealing and knee-shaking. Neither of us has the pluck to exhibit the bulges of fat before the youngsters, so we "mermaid" after dark. [...]

Mrs. Pop Shop is a blister. It's such a little step over to my camp. My fire is cosy and the animals all about it and Henry hopping about. So she comes and she stays long epochs of time. She doesn't sit but stands, first on one leg then on the other, and the fat of her sagging and the breath of her wheezing as her voice drones on and on and on. Unfortunately the "pop" trade is slump on these cold, dull days. Even the Rile-My-Biles don't linger but snort and whiz up and down the highway without stop. *[...]*

SEPTEMBER 2ND

Two woodcutters whom I call Death and Destruction annoy me very much. They race past the Elephant, kicking up dust and making horrid noises. It is terror for the dogs and one never knows where they are coming and going. It's a crime to let those wood trucks race through the park, cutting up the roads and messing up everything the way they do. What's the good of the beastly authorities?

Henry is lots better and very happy and lucid. I catch him singing or at least doing unmusical noises. I've shut down on too much Pop Shop blight. The boys were here in our midst all day, making all the dogs bark and swarming into everything. I had the outfit to supper last night and so discharged my full obligation to the tribe. She's an all-day sucker and the kids like sticks.

I have constructed myself a studio behind the van against the invasion of Rile-My-Biles on Sunday and the Labour Day holiday. I can't shut out their squeals and smells but at least they can't see me. It's too dark to work in the van. I did a good sketch this morning. I am beginning to settle my neck in the yoke and forge ahead, dragging my burden behind instead of trying to push it ahead and getting my harness all snarled up.

SEPTEMBER 3RD

It does my heart good to see Henry. He is so happy hearted and (for him) energetic and lucid—nearly normal. We joke along; he is eating and sleeping well too. One day of Rile-My-Biles is over. They were pretty thick and each brought out one or more dogs. My tribe had a dullness in them.

Well, I had just washed the dishes and self and was about to retire to the studio and work when "they came." I told them I was here and they might. Poor old dears. It is a little break in their snarling lives. The children go for each other as usual. I walked her among the cedars. She loved it all. Smoked incessantly and spat everywhere, her breath like a bad drain. She is always so ill used and thinks everyone is against her. She'd love to be out in camp with me. Oh, oh, oh! Cedars, cedars give me strength, ripe, mellow, subtle growth and tolerance. The old man loves Woo. Chuckles at her antics by the hour. I felt like a jelly bean that had fallen into hot water when they left.

OCTOBER

[...] When Mrs. McVickers was staying with me (thank goodness she is dotty about animals too), one morning she lifted a superfluous pillow from the dresser where it had lain all night and there was a small black rat. Most would have hystericked and screeched. She called me. He was all in, nearly dead, mashed and battered. It was obvious he had come in with the coal for the bin in the hall had been filled the day before. Well, I put him in Susie's box. They are not the local brown rats but frequent the wharves. Now there is white rat Susie and black rat Sammy. He is terrified of Susie, minds her much more than he minds me. Milk and food bucked him up and now it's the deuce. How can I resuscitate him and then murder him? He is quite beautiful, he and his God life, the only one life in him.

Edith and Henry are going. She told me last night and cried, for the problem of Henry is becoming acute. He is so sane in some ways and so idiotic in others. He has run wild for years, roaming where he will. The thought of shutting such a one up is dreadful, yet he needs someone to control him. Edith can't, [being] away at business all day. I can't; he does not live in my house but their own and resents intrusion. His days are spent in absolute nothingness. I feel if he only had some definite task, however light, it would be miles better for his mind and body. But who's to set him a job? You have to work with him every moment. I've tried it; the minute you leave, Henry sits down and quits. He can work but he can't stick. He hops on one foot all over the place. Thump, thump, thump. Thank goodness the lady below is out all day. It almost sends me crazy. He says he can't help it, but I feel it is his empty useless life that turns all his thoughts in on his nerves. It prods them into all these exasperating gymnastics; he rolls his eyes and his tongue to give one the whorlies. Yet withal he is perfectly sane.

OCTOBER 5TH

[...] I've been looking at A.Y. Jackson's mountains in the C.N.R. Jasper Park folder. Four good colour prints but they do not impress me. They might be done from photographs, magnificent subjects but decorative and commercial. *Now, I could not do one tenth as well but somehow I don't* want *to do mountains like that.* They don't feed or impress you, a look or two does. They have passed through his eyes but not his soul. His work never stirs me. It is easy enough to see for he is resplendent in illustration. Lots of it is interesting in colour and design, but it is not choice or subtle. *Shut up, me! Are you jealous and ungenerous? I don't think it is that.* Something about the man riles me. He has one of those noses I never get on with anyway.

Susie is making love wildly to Sammy but he is morose and will have none of her. I ought to get rid of him but it seems so low down; it bursts the lamp of hospitality to drown after you have entertained and cosseted the wounded beast back to life.

Three visitors to the studio tonight. They sat in a row like three flower pots full of dirt and nothing growing in them. Stodgy, oh my! If it had not been for Susie and the dogs I'd have sobbed myself to sleep in front of their three noses. And as they exited, the man moaned out, "Your things have simply thrilled me." Good Lord, if they take their thrills thus, how *do* they take their "bores"?

TRIP TO CHICAGO
1933

MONDAY, NOVEMBER 6TH

[written in Chicago]

[…] It is dark today, brooding and oppressed. The lake looks cruel, bottomless and hard. The wind has dropped and Chicago is still and sullen. No letters from Toronto or elsewhere. I did expect to hear today. My first letter to them was posted Thursday. Drat the mails! Or don't they love me up there any more and are indifferent alike to my woes and to my coming? Bess wished it was me coming for the Ex to stay with her instead of Sara Robinson — maybe she's found Sara far more entertaining and won't care if I never come. Can you wonder? Sara (I've met her) is young and attractive and clever and AMIABLE. *Bess has reason to know me for a spit-cat and Lawren will be up to his top hair in the exhibition and too busy to think of old me at all. Emily, don't you know by now that you're an oddment and a natural-born solitaire? There is no cluster or sunburst about you. You're just a paste solitaire in a steel claw setting. You don't have to be*

kept in a safety box or even removed when the hands are washed.
Tired, sick to death of Chicago and it's snowing. No word from
Toronto. What mails! Or is it the folks? Suppose I went without
hearing and Sara Robinson was there? It might be awkward for
Bess. But I'll go when the week is up here, letter or no letter.

NOVEMBER

[Written on the train from Chicago to Toronto, November 8–10]
Bathing beaches, statuary, monuments, parks, memorials,
churches, schools, universities, orphanages, Chinese quarters,
nigger quarters, Jews' quarters, factories, foundries, department
stores — all these on gigantic scales. Millions and millions and
millions of tons of brick and stone, miles and miles of parks. But
horrible, horrible. It was built up largely on blood — blood of innocent hearts — abattoirs. Chicago's glory and wealth producer —
blood! I was terrified we might go near the fearful carnage places
on tour, but we did not. I think he said there were over 1600 old
churches in Chicago. We visited the Elks' Memorial in honour
of the World War heroes, a lavish display. Maybe they do good in
raising one's thoughts but I wonder if it's not mostly a desire to
produce the best and the biggest monument. So much of the
town rolled out to us in terms of "millions" and "biggests" —
all sentiment seems crushed out by the ponderosity and money
values. Nigger town is enormous. It seems so strange, the impossible barrier. Both human developing, growing beings. Will the
gap ever be bridged? One does not see how it is possible. I can see
the American Indian falling in step with the white races and the
Eastern peoples — Chinese and Japanese — but I can't see the niggers. I like them but I don't feel sisterly exactly. [. . .]

There are mud icicles hanging under the motors. The railroad and motor road lie parallel and close. There is no privacy about these [workers'] homes; they stand bare and exposed on all sides. Your eye travels uninterrupted from their verandahless front door to the porchless back. The windows are like birds' eyes that do not wink their lids, and their one-point gable fronts remind one of old women with middle-parted hair. The empty houses look as desolate as the last year's birds' nests. The sun pretended he was coming out and then went in and slammed the door. I don't know where we are, in my country or their country, but it's one country—North America, one swell land!

The woman in front and the woman behind have amalgamated and are swapping experiences—children, jam-making, travel and operations. Neither is interested in the other's experiences but vastly so in her own. One is fatter than me and has great hands with fingers like bananas. Dead cabbages and cemeteries abound. It is not so flat. I'm sure I smell Canada. Ann Arbor—I never heard of Ann, so don't know if she's U.S. or Canada.

I've slept and cricked my neck something frightful. Dusk is falling and appetite rising. Bess and Fred and Lawren and the art show and talks almost in reach.

Gee whiz! Here's something most important coming—brick buildings, low and long and many, and fine paved streets. Ford Motor Manufacturers! What a wonderful man Mr. Ford is, a real worth whiler on the earth. My word, Detroit is some place—workshops of different kinds for miles and miles. To think of all the multimillions of things they make and send out to the ends of the earth, makes you worse than giddy biliousness. [...]

Seven hours more.

Mr. Snoopia and his satellites have rifled my bags for duty and given their gracious permission to continue on my way in peace. Here's Windsor, Ontario. Welcome, dear Canada! There's no snow and a nice sky bright in the West and a big dog racing free with a boy. I only saw three dogs in the States — those miserable specimens straining on a leash in city parks.

Is it immigration or is there a subtle difference since we crossed the borderline? We are only just across. The air is lighter and clearer — the women and men who got on at Windsor are not so smart in clothes and carriage. Hello, there's a picket fence; I did not see any in the U.S. (all wire or mostly nothing) and lots of trees, little planted ones and woods too and long rows of poplars. I thought the East was different to the West — now it seems the East and the West are the same and the other side of the line, the States, is different. [...]

London, Ontario. Had a mouthful of cool, clean Canadian air. I think of those lung charts at the Fair and feel mine are much prettier for it. Have been to the diner. Now we are slithering through black night and there is nothing further to be done than wait with occasional feeds of Whitman. [...]

NOVEMBER 10TH

[In Toronto]

[...] *Bess gave a lovely party, mostly artists but all were doers of things and thinkers. The room was not only full of them but what they did was there too. I knew a lot of them before and those I didn't I do now. They were all so awfully nice to me. I loved every one. It's a rare thing to be in a company of doers instead of blown-out air cushions. At home I want to sneak off and yawn. At this party I felt alive. Just one thing hurt* — those spaces on the wall where my pictures hung in the Group show. Such a feeling of dead failure! I felt that people were sorry for me because of my failure and I said to myself, "Old fool, drink this medicine. It is part of the game, bitter and necessary." So I gulped it, grinning. I have accepted it. Somewhere, somehow, I shall find what I'm after. It may not be yet or even here; it may only be by crushing humiliation, but what I want is there and if I stick and am sincere it WILL COME and can't be prevented. Maybe I hoped there'd be a clue hidden among all those Chicago new and old ones. No one can help me much, not even Lawren. No one can grow for another, not one; no one can acquire for another, not one — the struggle is in one's own soul.

NOVEMBER 18TH

[On the train from Toronto to Vancouver, via the United States] [...] How bored the people in the train are! Not one of them looks out. They shut themselves into their little compartments and try to take a tuck in time to get this passing from the East to the West over, to eat it past and sleep it past, remembering only the beginning and the end and not experiencing the glorious now of the middle.

Last Sunday evening Lawren Harris lectured in the Theosophy Hall on war. It was a splendid lecture but terrible, one of those dreadful things that we want to shirk, not face. He spoke fearlessly about the churches and their smugness, of mothers offering their sons as sacrifices, and the hideous propaganda of politics and commerce exploiting war with greed and money for their gods while we stupidly, indolently, sit blindfolded, swallowing the dope ladled out to us instead of thinking for ourselves. His lecture was mainly based on two recent books, No Time Like the Present *by Storm Jameson and another I forget* the title of. The preparations for war are fearful beyond belief. It took some courage to get up and tell people all that awfulness.

The weak sunshine is throwing long, long shadows. The Opposites have drawn their blinds and are spread out on their possessions, tossed like empty cans on garbage, filling their vacuum with sleep. Ah! One of their "goody" boxes has fallen and he has put his foot in it. This will be serious when she wakes, for I have observed she dominates.

I wish I was like a doll that can sit either way. I used to love to make mine sit with their back hair facing their laps and their hind-beforeness ridiculous. I loved to make my dolls look fools to get even with them for their coldness, particularly the wax or china ones. I loved the wood and rag much best. The wooden ones rolled their joints with such a glorious, live creak and the rag ones were warm and cuddly. But none of them could come up to a live kitten or puppy.

She's found out about their goody box. He has excused himself and gone quickly out.

Valley City! How can it be that! It takes hills to make a valley. Oh, I see it is unflat before and behind, though not so much but that the tombstones can peep over. Poor deads, I wonder if that is the highest they ever get. One last burst of sunshine is over the fields, gilding them. Our smoke is rolling behind in golden billows. There's a golden farm and a windmill and a golden cow and horse, but the richest of all in goldness and shameless shamming are the stacks of straw and chaff. The turkeys have gone to bed atop the barn roof, up above the icicles. How uncosy. It's getting so near Christmas that perhaps they've lost heart and think any old roost will do, poor dears! I'd rather barn roof and icicles than roasting pan and gravy, myself. Life is full of opposite contraries.

Mrs. Opposite's typewriter clacks furiously as if she must kill time at all costs. Maybe, like me, she's writing thoughts. Certain sure she doesn't catch them fresh out the window. But she may be full to the hat of canned ones, perfect fruit, well sterilized, pasteurized, hermetically sealed, labelled, sorted, carefully washed so that no bit has oozed out; while mine, being crude, unwashed and unsterilized, may mould and ferment, so that when I see them again they will have soured and I shall throw them out disgustedly like my pictures. Who judges? First thoughts are crude and immature, last ones sterile, dead. It is the sane, rational, middle thought that sits steady and keeps.

Now it's night and our guardian angel, "black as the night," is putting us to bed. He's at it when you return from dinner and the scrap of space which is yours by right of purchase is made yours by right of privacy. The uninspiring bald of the front man's head is shut out and the glassy stare of the behind woman's eye is shut out, and the "opposites" are shut up in their space which must be very small for him and her and their boxes and bags and typewriter. The steel bangles she wears rattle, and I hear, "Can't you get out of the way?" Poor soul, he couldn't, except by evaporation. We are not mingling or a friendly cargo. There is no communication between sections. Each has shut themselves tight into themselves. When night comes the car is ossified into solidity, the accumulation of pent-up thoughts and air and energy, the heating friction of tight packed, the lack of air and the abundance of heat, the glare of the lights, the smells of humanity and the thoughts pushing through the density ahead and the disturbance; the wheels and the swaying wiggle and the smoke of our engine outside make a great, solid unrest. The stops are too short to [do] more than fill one nostril and rest one foot on good Mother Earth before "all aboard" goes. There is one friendly, cheery soul aboard, the nigger waiter. He is so pleased when you tip him that you want to tip him again for being pleased and he hopes to see you again at dinner as if he really did. The porter is "lined with the same" and exhibits no tinge of a lighter hue, and here he is to make me up.

Mandan, North Dakota, and a breath of air. I went to buy a paper and handed the boy 25 cents I had got at dinner. "What kind is it?" he said and threw a shrewd eye over my coin and handed it back to me with, "Canadian — don't work any more," so I am newsless.

NOVEMBER 19TH

8 A.M. Montana, and the grandest kind of morning. The night was also grand. I was awake a lot. I think every star in the universe was out and was newly polished. The sky was high and blue and cold and unreachable. I'm glad I know now that that is not where we have to climb to find Heaven.

I like Montana, the going and coming of it and its up-and-downness. Lovely feelings sweep up and down the rolling hills getting tenser as they rise and terminate in definite rather defiant ridges against the sky. The sky itself does wonderful things, pretending to be the sea or to be under the earth, and to be unreachably high. It loves to wear blue and do itself up in little white pinafores and flowing scarves of many colours, and to tickle the tops of the mountains so that they forget about being rigid and defiant and seem to slide down the far side as meek as Moses. There's lots of cattle, heavy, slow-moving, bestial, black or red, with white faces and shaggy coats. The foolish square calves pretend to be frightened of our train.

Bluffers! Haven't they seen it every day since they were born? It's just an excuse to shake the joy out of their heels.

Livingston, and my feet have touched Montana. I've smelt and tasted it, keen, invigorating. Things here are much propped up and reinforced. There are myriads of clothes-pins all on the lines. I suspect the nippy wind of this morning is not unusual. We have gone through the Bad Lands in the dark again. It's not quite honest to put their fascinating queernesses on the railway folders and always slither through in the dark.

Mrs. Opposite has four great coats and a sweater in her own right and then there are all his. They have evidently "squared" the porter — he lets them keep their things billowing over into the aisle. At night they have the inside of their compartment draped in sheets and get extra blankets provided. Mercy! I'm roasted with one in the bunk, no extra blankets and the window open. She wears steel bangles that clank. I think she's all steel — like Rosie in "Tillie the Toiler." There seems to be a sisterliness between her and the typewriter. It sure doesn't get up to rebellious ruction like mine. She has just dropped her knitting needle — it too is steel.

Logan, Montana. I should not like to live here. The hills are clay-coloured rock with scrubby, undernourished trees. Lightning balls are on any houses of size.

One thing in the car is too friendly and interchangeable — the coughs and sneezes. They call to each other out of the compartments in a "hail fellow well met" way I do not like. There was a tiresome one kept up most of the night. I nearly took it some of my grapes for quincture but just as I was getting out of my bunk I wasn't sure whether it was masculine or feminine, so I ate the grapes.

The mountains are higher now, barren and a little cruel. I feel in my bones there will be beastly black tunnels soon. Nearly every house has a dog—no kind, just a leg at each corner, a head and tail back and front, but I bet inside they all have standard hearts. *It's Sunday and children and elders are doing things, playing, riding, driving, looking over cattle. There are a few out in automobiles, and one complete family is setting out for church with their books under their arms, and conscious of their best. There are magpies and pheasants and rabbits, occasionally flocks of turkeys and beehives. Tomorrow we will reach the far West. Gee, my back aches!*

I was in the diner when we came to those great plains before you get to Butte. We had been climbing for some time and were high up on queer mountains of odd-shaped boulders thrown together in masses. The train wound in and out among them groaning horribly as it took the curves. Down below was a vast, tawny plain with long winding roads and a few horses and cattle. Your eye went on and on and slowly climbed the low distant brown hills. I never saw anything like it before. It was not a space of peace but rather of awe. It seemed a great way before we saw queer built-up places and great mounds of slag, and scarred mountains with their bowels torn out and reservoirs and towns, and queer mining erections and cars of ore, all the ruin and wrack of man's greed for the wealth of the earth. We circled the great plain and went on through sagebrush. There would be a wonderful wealth of material for a certain type of painter here. Stunted little black trees and black cattle are scattered among the hills, and you can't tell which is one and which the other.

It has happened in the last half hour while I was asleep. I do not know it by the map but in my own self that the East is past and the West has come. As we came down from the hills the trees thickened. Now it looks not unlike what we went through but it is different and the last station was different and western. Mr. Opposite is having a turn at the typewriter. The sound is quite different under his pudgy fingers. She is arranging her suitcases. I miss the eastern sky—this one is low set and heavy. *Heavy fog has shut down and all we can see is the dim ground and tree roots—everything else is washed out.*

I have been reading "Song of Myself" by Walt Whitman. I am very tired. I think we of the West are heavier and duller than the Easterners. The air is denser and moister, the growth more dense and lush, the skies heavy and lowering. (My hair is all curly on the edges with damp.) Might not all this affect us too?

We will arrive in Seattle 8:30 A.M. tomorrow. I should be home by 1:30 if I connect. Beloved West, don't crush me! Keep me high and strong for the struggle.

NOVEMBER 20TH

All night the demon monster has rushed us into the West in a series of rough jerks and bumps, as if we lagged and it bullied. It is all West now, no trace of East left—low sky, dense growth, bursting, cruel rivers, power and intensity everywhere. I think it is a little crushing and then I note the fine trees, how straight they grow, not one kink or swerve in a million of them, plumb straight.

The Opposites went last night. The car is almost empty. The sniffs and coughs have gone. Blackie is mopping his face so hard, if it wasn't black through it would come off. I'm going home. Why aren't I tip-toppy and gay? I love home and my folks and the creatures. I love the West. It is the unpierceable mystery that baffles and discourages me.

The fusses are all finished. *Now I am on the boat. Here's a corner of the lounge where I can perhaps sleep away the time or part of it.*

Funny thing, there was not a moment to be lost on the train. I looked intently always. But the boat is different, just water and more water, and sky galore, and snatches of land here and there, but vague and not intimate. In the train you've got to look and think because you are all squeezed up. You've got to get out in some way, so you do—out the window with your thoughts and eyes. Otherwise you'd burst. But on board, people let their thoughts gape away over the sea, and gulls help. They take people out with them over the water unconsciously. There is so little life along the railway. When there is, it is mostly wild and scuttles too quickly to follow. The gull gives you time. Now we are bellowing and backing out and the gulls are folding up their legs preparatory and it's quite different from Chicago's Lake Michigan. Nor is it like Toronto. It's the dear, grand West and me, and I'm frightfully hungry. How queenly this ship is after the snorting, bumpity train. But the sea is restless; it has not the calm, pushing growth of the earth.

MOVING FORWARD
1933–34

DECEMBER 1ST

[...] Until one's thoughts have come through, how *can* one's pictures come through? And we are such shirkers. It is so easy to play vacant and slither around the corner and change the subject—but it's so *hard* to stand still and face it and search and search and search the thing 'til its bulwarks evaporate. Brag

and Bully won't do. You've got to plead and wheedle. You've got to beg and be let in humbly, not wormlike but humbly sincere.

DECEMBER 8TH

[...] I have just come off a three days' starve and feel fine. We eat too much. It is my cure for neuralgia and such-like pains. Orange and grapefruit juice only for three days. How clean and easy one feels after, gay as pyjamas on the line on windy wash days. Yet the weakness of me puts it off, making every excuse before starting in. When started, I generally stick.

When I woke this morning, someone was saying to me, "And now go forward; take your courage in your hands and let whatever will be, BE." Last night Susie the rat found her way upstairs to the bedroom. I felt something against my back and was startled awake. Susie was very pleased with herself.

DECEMBER 11TH

A letter from Lawren. He's a *real* person. How worth while friendship is when it is that unashamed kind that can talk straight of soul things and the deep things of one's work that really matter. Not just the froth of life, the fillings and surface. We have a compact between us that each will not deny his own Divinity, I mean state of yourself and your work. I used to, horribly, instead of recognizing and calling for the Divine in oneself. Oh I must lay aside all those little details of life that occupy me so much — clear the decks for action, keep my ideas straight and high and think over the heads of digging and dogs and dishpans, good in their places, but make them sit under the higher things, not occupying too prominent a place in life. Whitman says — everything is good in its place, bad is only good out of its own place.

DECEMBER 12TH

[...] Is theosophy good or bad? I wish I knew. Some of it seems splendid to me and some wicked. Love and mercy left out; law and justice predominate.

JANUARY 7TH [1934]

One's place of worship is that place where he draws nearest to the universal spirit — God — whatever leads him to that place is his religion. If it is music, or singing, or gardening, or painting, or any other thing that brings him into tune with God and with himself, that is the religion for him. No man can judge what is the religion for others, because the bodies themselves are aware of being in harmony. No one knows the best man's tune; that is why we three women are so different and can only go so far into each other. We don't know one another's tune. Yet I love them better than anything.

JANUARY 9TH

Last night I went to a lecture on the Mahatma Ghandhi by a Hindu, Raja Singh. It was splendid. [He was] well-educated, good-looking, vital and witty and charming, and he made me love the Mahatma Gandhi for his unselfish bigness. These Eastern men have SOMETHING behind them that we Westerners have not got. They make you feel so clumsy and material. Lee Nan does that too though he is quite an ordinary Chinese. Somehow they seem more in touch with the Eternal.

JANUARY 11TH

He [Henry] is getting very insolent. Poor little Edith. The selfish brothers go their own way, pleasuring. If there was only some hybrid between a lucrative asylum and a nursing home. He fits in neither. They are going to board [him]. I don't think that will last long; there is a nervous, fretful husband. I don't feel of any use. I have tried to be nice to Henry, to help him, but he's impossible. Perhaps I have not enough tact. Perhaps boarding with a family will be better. He will be with them more.

Oh Lor'! My other sister has been to see the sketches. I am in no wise puffed but pancake flat. She insisted that my forest was a waterfall. The only thing that impressed her was the amount of stuff.

JANUARY 29TH

I have said goodbye to the Raja. He's splendid. I heard him eight times and I am so glad he came here — I can't tell how glad. My whole outlook has all changed. Things seem silly that used to seem smart. I have decided to take my stand on Christ's side, to let go of philosophers and substitute Christ. I wrote to "Uncle Raja" (that's what his Eurasian children call him) and he gave me a beautiful "May God bless you" as I took his hand and said goodbye tonight after the lecture on Mahatma Gandhi. Oh, I do want the kind of religion that he offers — it is verily of Christ. [...]

How can I describe this man of God, Raja Singh? He is so simple; no arts, no affectation or self-consciousness. He looks like a simple boy when he enters the church with the attending parson. His hair is black, skin dark. I do not know if he is handsome or not. That is one thing about people I put in my garden down in my heart. I have noticed that I do not remember their outside appearance, but their inside looks only. I forget their features. I think that is my test whether they belong to the garden, because it is a garden for souls, not for outsides. I generally remember their hands. Raja Singh's hands are very long and slender Indian hands. He has a plain little black Testament and he holds it close so tenderly as if he loved it. When he prays, it is a swift thing as though he met God immediately. He prays aloud very little. When he does, the words come slowly and few, but every one counts. He speaks to a near God and a real one. Nobody coughs or sneezes. God is too close. They have not settled down for a dry ten minutes of supplication that must force its slow way through interminable space to dump its burden gasping somewhere near God. He closes his eyes and instantly God is there in the midst of us. The amen is swift as if the message he had through prayer would not wait but must pour forth; out it comes without hesitation, gaining volume and power as it proceeds. I cannot imagine anyone sleeping under Raja Singh.

Perhaps my wanderings among Eastern philosophies have given me a better understanding and quicker grasp of Easterners. Surely it has been a journey of many steps but each one has taught me. I can see it as I look back now. I have been led on. In a stray newspaper I found the name of Raja Singh and I knew I was to go. There was an art lecture the same night. I had been asked to go even by the lecturer himself (Mr. Vanderpant from Vancouver). Then by mistake, friends called for me and brought me to the art lecture instead of Raja Singh. It would have been easier to go in, but I had to go to the other. God led. Had I been disobedient, what I would have missed.

Raja Singh is neat and smart in outer appearance as though the clean orderliness of his inner life showed right through him to the very last layer of his clothing in a godly self-respect. He is vital and emphatic to a terrific degree, yet does not rant and screech and denounce. He mentions neither Heaven nor Hell.

His theme is Christ. I asked him about after death. "I am not sure," he said. "God looks after that. I can trust him. I have to live in the present the best I can like a little child, leaving things safely with the father." Or words to that effect.

Raja Singh is courteous, honest and sincere. He said nothing of my pictures when he stood before them. I felt them empty and I loved and honoured him more because he did not hypocrite, pretending that they meant anything to him when they did not. He thinks very much of his friend "E. Panters's" work, is very proud of him. He graduated and won a scholarship from the Royal Academy schools and studied in Italy. He said that Panters's work was greatly influenced by the Italian school. It is good to have the lustre ripped off your work. The flavour is bitter when you know nothing has registered—there is only a blank. Uncle Raja says, "You cannot take anything out of an empty pot." And these silly people praise empty canvas and call them "spirituality."

What does spirituality in painting mean? First, the seeing beyond the form to the spiritual reality underlying it—its meaning. Second, the determination, power and courage to stick to the ideal at all costs, but there is a danger of letting the ideal become diluted with vagueness, uncertainty, indecision; then the thing is lost and left unsaid. Uncle Raja is practical. He has tired of the visionary circles—like a child he has come to ask for bread and butter—honest plain things. He demands no fantasies and selfish shutters-up-of-themselves, but letting the light of Christ in the heart where it should radiate to others about you. No noisy snivelling surrenders, no holding hands up and going on your knees and shouting your emotions. He leads to Christ and leaves them there at Christ's feet and Christ will take care of them.

That is how they do [it] with the Eurasians. They show them but they do not sit underneath them to hold them up. They teach them to use their own faculties and to take their perplexities to God for guidance. Did not Walt Whitman say, "No one can grow for another, no one / No one can acquire for another, not one."? You've got to rely on God and on yourself, not on other people. Right through your life be strong, not flabby.

He has phoned to say goodbye and to give me his blessing. He has left a book at the YMCA for me to read. He has made me feel India is just across the street, almost within shouting distance and well within the praying radius. Tomorrow he goes to Seattle and then into [the] southern states and eastern Canada and New England, and possibly home via Victoria in 18 months' time. Bless him and his work always, and now I look around to see what effect all this will have on my work. Will it make it more vital? Or will it—finish it. Or—I leave it to God and watch to be told. This has stirred me to the foundations. I am exhausted today for I have been wrenched this way and that, lifted, thrown down, rejoicing, despairing. Oh when this ferment wears off, will I find peace and surrender finally, or will I be rooted and stand firm and end this 50-year chase? Go back to my starting point, for I believed and loved God then, though I was a bit scared of him too.

Now, little book, because I write so much about Uncle Raja, do not think the wrong way that it is just the man, his personality. It is all that lies behind. It is the eternal search, it is the hope that my searching is about to arrive at a goal. Maybe it's the joy in the sight of home after fifty years of looking for a new location, and if I go into detail about the Raja it is because I want to be sure in myself how I stand in regard to this thing that he preaches and he is. I want to get it clear so that if I should slacken up I can review, as it were, this whole thing; that if I am nodding, it may prick me awake, to remember my first reaction clearly.

My sisters took the Raja each in her own way. Both were invited to meet him the first night he came to my house, but as he had to leave after supper, they did not see him. One sister wanted to see what manner of missionary could be interesting to me (the family black sheep). She went to hear him when he lectured in her own church, and when he spoke on British Israel, said she was not impressed. She likes missionary addresses well sprinkled with the salt of Heaven and profusely peppered with Hell, and for folks to snivel up front and confess pathetically and all the harrowing deathbed stories of repentance, so that people quiver and squeal over them; [without that] she feels nothing is doing. The other sister seldom bothers over lectures. Her quaint prosaic religion satisfies her. Why stir up trouble? But she also went the night it was in her church, was mildly enthusiastic but did not go again 'til I invited her. Sunday night we sneaked off in a cab when Sister No. 1 was safely housed. It was a splendid meeting and my sister was impressed enough to go again herself next night. How did one mother and father produce three such antipodes in daughters?

Uncle Raja left a letter for me. In it he said this, "The Lord bless you and prosper you in every way and give you much of his joy and peace in the creative work he is using you to do. He is LIFE, LIGHT and LIBERTY." Perhaps then he did realize I was struggling really for something definite. I am sure I shall paint deeper and fuller for this experience and when I have let Christ fully take me for his own. In speaking of this opening up of oneself to let Christ in, Uncle Raja said it is the same way with human love. You know how you say, "Here I am, all of me, come in to every corner of me, here I am," so you should feel letting the Christ into your heart and life, open up feeling and shut him out of no corner.

I have written to Lawren and told him about things, I think he will be very disappointed in me and feel I have retrograded way back, fallen to earth level, dormant, stodgy as a sitting hen. I think he will hardly understand my attitude for I have been trying these three years to see a way through theosophy. He, Fred and Bess all tried to help me and wanted me to get it and become one of them. *Now I turn my back on it all and go back sixty years to where I started, but it is good to feel a real God, not the distant, mechanical, theosophical one.* I have read *The Sadhu*, Uncle Raja's book. It is beautiful and simple. Anyone could understand. Theosophy is so vague and whirling, just ordinaries cannot get that. *I am wonderfully happy and peaceful.* Dare I really let go? Has Christ come in to stay?

Last night I learned that dreadful horrible thing about poor Lizzie. I am glad she has told us and asked us to help. She is such a good soul! I just can't bear it. Those are the places Christ helps. He did last night.

God, God, God! Oh, to realize so completely that you could utterly let go and passionately throw your soul upon the canvas.

FEBRUARY 3RD

I think it's this way. Don't hunt out big people. Let them hunt you, if you are small ones, because maybe you can help them a little.

I am an expectant mother making clothes for the baby that is coming. Whether I feel like it or not I must paint every day, so that when the child comes, I will have something to clothe her in. Suppose she came and I had nothing ready and my body had to go naked and died of exposure and cold? It behooves me to make them fine and careful, these coverings, that my child may not be dressed in sackcloth and slovenly workmanship and people will laugh and turn away from the ugly thing. And oh, if it were stillborn—if the idea I have been searching for for so long materialized in my mind and I let it die there and did not bring it further with expression, but, idle and indifferent, let it fade and dwindle prematurely, that would be worst of all. The idea is God. Our part is to nourish and mother the idea, love it, cherish it and in due time produce. [...]

FEBRUARY 5TH

I have heard from Bess and Fred about my stories. Bess gives them but passing mention and goes on off up into theosophy. Fred tries to give me a straightforward honest crit. Both think my material good but my approach and construction *very* bad. I worked hard on these things but evidently to little purpose. Fred's exposition is not very illuminating. I think I must leave writing alone. That is, I must write for the bottom drawer, that's all, just to elucidate things for myself and ease up one's burstings, thoughts that press you too hard. Yet I wanted to show the animal side. Fred says why not let the animals autobiograph [and tell their own story]. That's twaddle. Animals do [not] expound except by their reaction on us.

FEBRUARY 7TH

I was wrong, unjust from soreness. *Fred's crit is fine, and kind too. He was honest with me and, oh goodness, how few people are! It's a compliment when people don't think you want "eye wash" as Fred calls it. He says there's too much* me, *too much* originality *(I suppose he means striving for effect, I did not know I had done that). I'll at them again and try and unify and concentrate and build to a pyramid and unhitch my horse and put him before the cart and cast out* me *and seek to find expression for the wordless subtlety of the beasts. He says I must live and experience my stuff. Heavens! I thought I did. They swamp me at times but I haven't got connection between the thing and its equivalent in words.* Gee whiz! Just the same as in painting, just the same as in our religion; our profession and our action don't hitch up. There's a gap. I've written to Fred and I've told him about my going back to Christianity; that's off my chest. Our letters are all so full of work and theosophy. He and Bess and Lawren have been very good when I was in the dark heap; they'd like me to have seen things in the light of theosophy, and I thought I wanted to too, but it goes round in circles and makes you giddy and doesn't lead you, a sort of endless voyage with God always way way beyond catching-up distance. Just stern inexorable law without the love of a *real* Jesus Christ to bridge the gap; only a cold example. Christ is not a sinner's saviour. I have been reading *The Sadhu.* I love the Christ he shows. I want him for my own.

The snapping of this theosophy bond will make a difference to my beloved friends in the East. They all do so believe in its teachings. I wonder if it will cut me completely adrift from them. But I am glad to be back again and have peace in my heart. Alice is much interested in Raja's message also. That and this dread thing hanging over Lizzie's head is bringing us closer together.

FEBRUARY 12TH, 6 A.M.
[...] I went to wish Lee Nan Happy New Year. He is a funny little fellow. His place was so spick and span. He gave me some fearful sweetmeats—salt and bitter—and a Chinese orange, all pith and withered. He had a new picture. A large Chinese girl semi-nude with chrysanthemums behind her. I thought she was horrid, a mixture of English and Chinese mongrel painting. If he would only stick to his own fine way that has

such charm, but he wants to learn the English way. You can't discuss clearly with him because of his poor English. I am so much more at home talking of his Chinese things than his English ones. I can unreservedly admire them.

MARCH 3RD

[...] Miss Auld's art lectures at the Empress are good. She knows a lot and speaks well and looks fine. Her head shape and the way her hair fits on and is piled at the top back and on her forehead is nice. She spouts for nearly two hours with no notes, but—I sleep solidly the last third of the lecture. It's too long, especially for history. I like *is* of things more than *has been*, though I s'pose it's the has beens that make the is. Some of the slides I got great joy out of. Where you see the spirit of the painters shining through, that's more than hearing about them. What you hear may be true or not. The historians garble, may dilute or bloat the man, but [it] is the spirit of him that comes out in his painting, there [are] no frills or lies and no juggling. It is there or it is not there. It is what was in the man.

MARCH 7TH

There now! It doesn't pay to try to be nice. Mortimer Lamb asked to come to the studio and I said, "I will try and be decent and amiable and helpful to him." So I tried and I rattled out millions of canvases and sketches, which is hard, tiring work. Result—"I **have** *enjoyed myself so much. May I look* **again** *before I leave," says Mortimer. He's all keen on having an exhibition of my stuff in London. (They'd never accept it.) "It's a shame to think of you stuck out here in this corner of the world unnoticed and unknown," says he. "It's exactly where I want to be," says I. And it is, too. This is my country. What I want to* *express is* here *and I love it. Amen!* Mortimer Lamb seemed to feel my work quite deeply. He is an old man, did a little in his youth, and a lot of article writing on art etc. A funny old duck.

I've been reading Lawren and Bess's letters over. They are both exceedingly nice. I wonder if theosophy and its distant beauty and its cold aloofness from life and humanity really satisfies them — serene and joyless — and vague. They feel it bigger and higher than Christianity. *[…]*

MARCH 10TH

Oh that flat tyre woman — I am like a dishrag today. She rolled back and forth over my naked body with her mindless tyres and jammed all the juice out of me. I was too tired for inspirational work so delved in the garden. Meant to take my lunch to the beach and work but was too fagged and procrastinated instead. Going down late afternoon. Empty and flat as "Jean Auld" herself. I made myself weed a path and card a box of wool. Ran down to Alice's and encountered Una — after twelve years. I did not mean to run into her and wish I had not; was unprepared. The woman is ill. I'm sorry, but even so, can't go back to *feeling* her a relation. She [missing fragment] when she wrote that letter hoping I would die — I did to her and deads are deads. I do not feel ill towards her, just dead. Could not kiss her. Could not be Aunt Millie, but I'm darn sorry she's sick.

MARCH 13TH

Una Boultbee is still in town and I have seen little of my sisters during her stay. They are crazy over this niece of theirs. So I am an outcast and orphan these days. Am I such a very jealous person? I do not think I care a bit that they like her so much but sometimes

I wish they liked me a little more. If I am sick, they are very good to me — duty — but [if] I am well I don't count a row of peas in their lives [however] much they'd use the peas. Me they think only a painter. They are both so completely wrapped in their own affairs, other people's children and other people's ailments. If I go to them, all right — if I don't, why all right with them too. Loneliness has bitten my very soul at times. If ever I have rebelled, they have called me selfish, so I have gone to the animals and the woods. They have been the real company, though I do love my sisters and ache for their fellowship. I suppose everybody in the world is lonely sometimes. Far be it for me to want to be cluttered up always with human society, that would be worse than being lonely, *far*, only it's the perpetual aloneness that hurts.

MARCH 20TH

[...] I've been wrestling with the crow story. It came grudgingly and hard, as if the innards of the crow did not want to be exposed. I loved the crow and I say to myself, what do I want to show and say and express? Where did that crow and I touch? What good did I get from the crow, and what good did it do the crow kingdom that he lived intimately with humans?

A heavy fog hung around all day, and on top of the roof the din of reshingling. It seemed the nails were being driven right into my pate and when Wopper gave an incessant yap, I went down and spanked. After an early supper, the beach. Cold as the pole, steely blue sea and low sky, everything smashed flat and hard. I will work my sketch tomorrow as I did yesterday's today. Got it stretched and aligned and then clothed it in paint 'til its fairness was smothered as a nun beneath her draperies. I would that my touch was not so cowlike. More tender and gentle, not slippery.

MARCH 26TH

[...] Why is Lizzie so intolerant of my deafness? She is always saying, "Why don't you listen?" or that I am stupid. She doesn't bother to speak clearly to me and is the most difficult of any voice I know to catch. I go down wanting companionship and come back nettled. That's what's weighed me down today. I went down to chat while they were at lunch and wished I had not. Now I must dive into the crow story.

MARCH 30TH

Have finished the crow story, "Sandwich." I wonder if it is any good. One thing I do know, I've sweated over it with all that's in me.

APRIL 5TH

[April 5 is the date in *Hundreds and Thousands*, but it is April 11 in the manuscript]

Lawren asked if he could see the "Cow Yard" so I posted it today. He will pass it on to Fred. I told Fred and Bess about it before I told Lawren, but they have neither said to send it and they have not answered my letter. Bess is no good as a critic — not really helpful, but Fred is. He slashes and doesn't care how he bruises or damages your conceit. Lawren is too kindly, doesn't smack hard enough to be stimulating. *[...]*

SUNDAY

[...] The little lily in my bedroom is such a joy. The bloom has passed its prime and is going downhill. Bess's favourite flower and very typical of her — white, still, remote, a little hard and unyielding. Theosophists are a little *un*human. More like Calla

Lily than the Madonna, which is all curves and perfume. God, God, God. It is not religion we want, it is YOU.

APRIL 22, 1934

[...] Listening to Clem Davis last night gave me the woollies. What is one to do? Must they look continually at the awfulness and the dirt when they can't do anything? Why not look at the unattainable loveliness of spring in its full beauty and put the rest from us — facing it when we must, trying to live our best always but keeping our eyes on the beauty, not on the horror, just as long as we can? Even when the horrors do roll over us, if we are full of lordliness perhaps they won't crush so hard.

Now little journal — diary — whatever you call yourself, let's see if I can clarify my thoughts a little through you, defacing your white surface to clean up some hazy muddle below the surface. This painting business and its aims. One thing's sure, as in life, so in art: everyone has their own problems and they must be worked out by that person. We are all so terrifically alone in our big things: birth, death, religion, art. The other fellow can come with you to the steps, but you have to mount those steps and go in alone.

First, I got a lot of help from those in the East. The last two years I have had none. I do not know if it is their fault or mine. They say nothing of value. Bess found fault with the shape of my picture and the frame. No help in that. Lawren had nothing to say. No more has he any comment to make on the "Cow Yard." Bess comments on the stories I send over. "I have read and enjoyed the stories," nothing constructive about that. She and Fred have had the "Cow Yard" three weeks now. Long enough, surely, for her to comment. He may be busy. Well, what do you write for? To please folks who aren't interested really, or to something within yourself? Or to let off steam, or to kill time, or a craving for expression, or something bigger than oneself trying to creep through the clay? Or is it the creative force, the God in us manifesting itself? But we are always so busy peeping to see what our neighbours are doing and to appropriate his thoughts, we forget to develop our own. What's more, if he isn't doing our way, we think he's wrong; and if he does our way, we call him a copycat, and there is no sense to us at all.

One thing I pay strict heed to, if you get a hunch about a work in a dream, try to follow it up. My last one was in regard to ensemble. The picture must contain one movement only and the articulations of that movement are very important. The eye must travel through the spaces without a jot or jolt. Earth, sky and sea must travel the same way. The end of their journey is the same destination. Your picture must not stop any more than life must. When it stops, it dies. It may run or climb or roll or dance, but it must not lie down and sleep. From the land, the movement sweeps out over the sea and up to the air. Its movement and its speed are one, and the more complete the movement, the more complete the picture. When you find the thing's direction in space, you find its key.

APRIL 24TH

[...] I believe language is the whole bother. People mean the same, the big thing is there sitting behind the silly little words that they voice differently. Take prayer, i.e., communion with God. Some call it going with the "silence," some say "quiet time," and some say "inspiration," and there are other words too, and some don't say anything or call it anything but pray all the same and perhaps better. Birds pray when they toss off the

very joy of life that is in them out into space to meet God, for God fills all space and He must recognize His own. A baby's chuckle means the same, and the complete content of a cow chewing her cud and the waggle of a fish in the sea; he does more waggle than he needs to just swim, the extra waggle is just like prayer. The joy God put in him speaking to God, words don't matter. It's only the lifting that counts. [...]

It's queer how things are. You have a friend who you think understands   they've made out they do. You show them something seems to you very plain and they don't understand at all, and an unreasonable annoyance springs up in you, and you don't know if you're disgusted with them or you, and you're like a cat after its own tail. One end says catch me, and the other end of the same cat says leave me alone. You want the person to understand, yet you don't want to have to explain. Oh shucks!

The gurgly bird goes on and on. His song has no beginning and no end. He just gurgles on as though it was no effort and he had to get so much gurgling in per day. As far as a bird's song can be dull and uninspiring, I think he is. No pep, no inspiration.

MAY 3RD

I have been to Vancouver to be on the judging committee of the Art School Graduates Association for their show, and I have also seen Sophie. [...] Sophie's visit was satisfactory and happy. She was watching at her window, the curtain drawn back, and her one eye and her toothless gums expressed everything they were capable of. I love Sophie's smile of welcome. It is just as dear, perhaps dearer, now that her countenance is abbreviated by losses; her heart seems to have grown bigger. "I have watched all day, yesterday, today and tomorrow for you," she said, and took me into the tiny front room Frank calls Sophie's Office. It has a tiny table where the little china Virgin and saints sit, a bunch of red and yellow paper roses in vases, and the walls are smothered in religious chromos and photographs of all her offspring who lived long enough to be photographed, the four who lived to ages between 2 and 12, [in] large ornate gilt frames with convex glasses. And a visit is not a visit unless these four are alluded to in some way. There is a frontless cupboard where a few clothes hang, mostly Sophie's favourite plaid skirts. There are two boxes and one wooden chair, and some baskets for sale carefully tied in dust cloths. The little low window looks out onto mud flats with a built-up rail track across what used to be the Indians' own beach. Wharves, boathouses and mills have pushed the reserve back rudely. The Indian houses are helter-skelter, the lots are overgrown with rank grasses and everybody has a few cherry trees, old and gnarled. The houses are always changing. Sara Denny found hers too large so she cut the front off, and I couldn't recognize it, and walked up and down the street searching. Sophie is always moving the partition in hers according to the moment's fancy. When I knew her first, it had three rooms. Shortly after, it only had one. "You have a new house," I said. "Oh no. Three rooms with three stoves. So I cut out the walls and made one room so one stove would do." Another time she divided it into four. At present it is divided into two.

The stove moves all over the house and shoves its smokepipe out of any window or hole that is handy. Should they move it in any corner where there is not a hole, Frank cuts one. Sometimes there are iron bedsteads, and sometimes the mattresses are on the floor and the bedsteads are sitting out under the cherry trees. And if Sophie is ill, that is generally the time Frank takes to paint her bedstead a new colour, and she lies behind that cosy stove on the floor. She tells me she is old fashioned and likes the ground best. Spring beds don't stay still, they move when she does and make her whole body sore moving every time she does. Dear Sophie and I are so happy when we are together. There's something very close between us. She gave me a beautiful basket. I did not like to accept it, she is so hard up, but she said, "Someday Sophie die. Then I like Emily have my basket and see me."

Movement is the essence of being. When a thing stands still and says, "Finished," then it dies. There isn't such a thing as completion in this world, for that would mean Stop! Painting is a striving to express life. If there is no movement in the painting, then it is dead paint. If the striving for and the longing for completion were satisfied, that would mean stagnation. A picture by a satisfied artist hangs lifeless on the wall, but if the artist is pulled with longing and striving to get on further — see beyond, keep moving — there will be a carrying on. Also for the beholder who himself will feel the need of pressing on further to something bigger, longing is greater than satisfaction. The taste of good is better when the appetite is keen and vigorous; when the stomach is heavy and full, inertia and drowsiness follow. You can't stand still, so keep moving forward for fear of rolling back.

One must be very spiritual indeed — or very young — to fully appreciate the cold dawn. To rheumaticky bones it brings aches and shivers the marrow. It needs a very strong soul to hoist itself above these.

MAY 7TH

Every bit of colour has rushed to the earth's face with an apoplectic rush. Green, green, it gives out the gripes. Bushes and

trees are overcrowded with leaves. The boulevards are full of
pink and white in May. So pink and so white that the leaves
scarcely show. Beacon Hill is vulgarly high scented and yellow
with bloom. Everything is superlative and lush with the heavy
rain. Only the garden keeps on weeding.

NOAH'S ARK
1934

MAY 15TH [Esquimalt Lagoon]
[...] How delightful it is when creatures stay near you for the
joy and pleasure of your company, not because they must. It's
dogs' nature to stay by their owners, but take Susie the rat and
Woo the monkey. They run around loose but tied by invisible
ties, the same invisible ties that tie us to our God, the very
same principle always at work.

MAY 22ND
[...] No letters from the East yet. I wonder if it's happened, the
inevitable mysterious something L[awren] has hinted at. I do
not want to conjecture for I may be wrong and think injustices.
Bess could drop a line even if F[red] is too busy. She claims to
be fond of me. There is one spot though where we are somehow
out of touch and sympathy; she no doubt feels as I do and neither could probably say just what it is — at present. Maybe it is
connected with the thing that is about to or has happened.
Maybe it's religion, maybe not.

Susie has the freedom of the world out here bounded by the sunrise and sunset. Susie's pink nose sticks up and smells the beyond. But Susie's world is bounded by the smell and sound of her old Mom. Susie's love of me tethers her within that radius. How strange and wonderful creatures are.

MAY 29TH

[...] I got a pot of tea and a hot bottle, for it was very cold, and I put the fire out with water and cosied the creatures down into their boxes, took food in the van and tucked into bed. [...] And read a letter from Bess. Apparently she had not been interested enough to even read the "Cow Yard." She said Fred had not had time to, otherwise she did not mention it. All right Old Girl (me). You've learnt your lesson. They've had it nearly two months. Funny, if I was interested in anybody (and they always make out they're interested in my doings), I'd want to read or see anything they did. It makes one doubt people's sincerity and it's jolly good for one's conceit.

Searching, searching.

JUNE 11TH

[...] The field is full of dandelions, energetic people always doing something, turning their clear yellow faces this way and that as the sun moves, wagging their heads in the wind, growing fearfully fast and hauling their green caps over their faces at night. My host says they are not dandelions, anyhow, they're one of the family. He calls moss "fog." It does take the Scotch to call things by their queernesses. There, 11:30 P.M. and nothing done but chores, religious exercise and my little write. Writing does help to clarify one's thought jumbles and express, but you can only express along the highway. The best things are off the highway. Sometimes there

is not even a trail and you have to break through. Those places are mostly inexpressible places that won't word. They are the best places but you are dreadfully apt to get lost. Perhaps if one goes on practising one may learn to word them.

JUNE 16TH

[...] There is no right and wrong way to paint except honestly or dishonestly. Honestly is trying for the bigger thing. Dishonestly is bluffing and getting through a smattering of surface representation with no meaning, made into a design to please the eye. Well, that is all right for those who just want eye work. It seems to satisfy most people, both doers and lookers. It's the same with most things — the puppies, for instance. People go into screams of delight over them — their innocent quiet look, their fluff and cuddle, but when the needs of the little creatures are taken into consideration they are "filthy little beasts" and a nuisance. The love and attraction goes deeper than the skin. You've got to love things right through for all that's good and bad, all they enclose. And in painting, you try to get all the space encloses and what the objects enclose, the thing common to all, what they toss back and forth from one to another. The relationship of each to each, the strong forces that have combined to make theirs separately and as a whole. And others, when you've got them all related as whole, you turn around and discover [each] object's own individual past. When you've decided its use and part of the whole, then you tie the parts all together and forget the bits, thinking only of the whole collection of bits and what they represent, and see the hand of God and listen to the voice of God in and through that very thing.

Suck, suck. That strenuous pulling at their mother's life that goes on perpetually in the corner of the van. You wonder how the old girl stands it, as if she stood aside and became only a sieve for life to pass through. With new puppies, her whole being is handed over to them. Voraciously they lap up her life. Mothers are life spreaders, yet they take keen joy out of their maternity, the instinct to keep things going push that is stronger than life itself.

Littlest pup of litter born in the Elephant, sick and crying. At daybreak of the second night I crept out and got a bucket of water and drowned the little pup. It was hateful but I couldn't bear to hear his cries of pain any longer. Pneumonia evidently. He was too young. I fed him cream and water every ½ hour but he was too weak to suck. There always seems such a uselessness in a young thing being born just to die. Now he lies under an enormous pine and I suppose the ants will clean him up quickly and grow fat . . . why should he be born for the ants? And why did he have to suffer? And had I the right to end his life? Why why why. The sun pulled the blue sky high up to itself and browned the wind up and it's lovely. [. . .]

HOPES AND DOLDRUMS
1934–35

JUNE 23RD, 1934

[. . .] Fred sent back the "Cow Yard." His crits were meagre and foolish. Found the story *very good* but bad spelling and grammar. He said nothing helpful to me. If spelling and grammar were pulled up, I might be able to sell it, but gave me no hint as to where to try.

Oh life! How queer you are. How should I write it? How explain the jolt a letter brought me today? "Judge not that ye be not judged." None of my business people loving one and living with another; that cannot be square and right. People married and living together in fiction cannot be right either. By and by we shall know.

Dream. The sky and the earth are one. The light pours down, is lapped up by the greatest sea and absorbed by the receptive earth. All runs through, all the same to express the oneness and allness. Moving, living, being together, to surround everything with atmosphere, to show the direction of its thought and growth, to show that thing coming and going, breathing through the object's life, to become a part of it yourself and feel its life and growth as your own life and growth, and the sunshine and the night passing through you also, and the lift and lilt of praise pouring through, filtering and rising up again like a mist.

JULY 9TH
[...] Bess is coming West. I don't know why.

JULY 11TH
[...] Tomorrow I go to Vancouver to meet Bess. She wired [she] is going back Saturday and wants to save her time. I almost wired back "go to the devil" but concluded the message would not take the right inflection on the wire. I'm fed up with Bess's antics, deceit and insincerity. Perhaps I'll know more when I see her and feel different. I feel as if the parting of our ways has come.

JULY 13TH

Yesterday, asking me to meet Bess in Vancouver instead of her coming to me. It was a disappointment. I was looking forward to having her in my house and showing her my sketches. So many things I wanted to show and share, but I went by the 2:15 boat and writing strenuously all the way up to have my work ready for class next morning. There were two funny old ladies aboard, both very deaf. They each had an electric contraption to hear within neat boxlike cameras. I looked up just as the two fell into adjacent seats and one asked the other a question. One was old and one was very old. The very old prided herself on being 80% deaf and over 80 years old, and the old one belonged to the Salvation Army, I expect. When Old asked Very Old, V.O. made a mad scramble among shawls and parcels and produced her box. The Old, not to be outdone, fished out hers from her seat back, and they compared and tried each other's and dumb showed and shouted and exchanged instruments and got so excited they missed instruments and put ears to mouths and mouths to ears and shook their heads and mouthed and finally put their instruments away and wrote. Seeing I was interesting, they included me, and our notes played merry-go-round. The last I saw of them, they were standing in the moil of embarkation. Their contraptions were put away, each stood alone in her own silent world.

Bess and a male cousin of Fred's met me. Bess strokes me the wrong way and sparks flew like black cats at night. She was all in grey and very pleased with herself and made eyes at the cousin. We went to the hotel which was horribly hot, and Bess sent wires for half an hour while I got madder and madder every time I shifted my weary feet. When she came back, I was cross and horrid and said when our time together was so short, why not have done that before I came, and she got a little nasty too and asked if I'd rather not hear the truth. I came up to here with her, and her eyes were rather sparky and looked straight like Woo's when she is mad. Let's get out of this beastly hotel, I said. It was stifling. Where can we go?

I suggested the park and we got a cab and did not say much. We each looked out of our windows — drove to the teahouse. It was glorious on the verandah under the great trees, and we eased up and she told me the whole story. It's rather horrid seeing life messed up that way. I'm glad they are out in the open now. They ought to have done it sooner. They've been living falsely. I don't feel that about Lawren. He was as frank with me as he could be, but I feel it about Fred and Bess. I feel as if I could never trust them again. I felt that the real friendship Bess and I had enjoyed was gone. I tried to be absolutely honest and frank with her. I told her that for many months I felt she had had no interest or part in my life. Nor had she let me into hers. Her eyes got cold and hard and sparky and horrid again. She asked me why I had asked in a letter to Lawren, "Is Bess sincere?" and I said I supposed it was because underneath I felt that she was living one life and acting another. We stood a long time by the stream entrance, looking hard at each other. I guess our paths spread apart now. I said we were apart now in the two great things — religion and art. And I asked if she and Lawren were going to work, and I wondered if the life would come back into his painting. I said it had grown dead and lifeless. It is still beautiful in colour and light but it did not live, and she did not like that. They are down in California getting divorces and consoling each other meantime. She prattled about higher love and non-sex and made me a little sick.

I was wrought up and exhausted when I got aboard. The door of the jolly old Eastern friendship has banged to, leaving them on one side and me the other. It's a little sad.

JULY 22ND

It is all very perplexing this life we live — discerning between the straight and the crooked. A Jew lives next door. He is not a nice man. I have only had one encounter with him and that over the phone about our mutual interests in the dividing fence. The Jew was horrid. His gait and his face and his voice all ill bred. His garage is up against my fence. When I am dressing in the morning, he is backing his car out. From my high window I do not see his face but I see two ghastly white claw-like hands on the wheel. They are cruel horrid hands. He gives terrible loud drunken parties. They get drunk and scream and come out and in the door and talk loudly and bang car doors and wake us all up from midnight to three and four. Once a man from my house went over and remonstrated, and once I wrote a courteous letter asking him to be quieter as it was interfering with my business. After that he was worse. Now I've put it in the hands of the police. He has women there all the time, painted hussies, beautifully dressed. They are loud and vulgar. One spent the night there last night. She has amber hair and painted cheeks and lips. The voice came out of her mouth like gravel from a steam shovel. She bared herself, all but a little pair of bathing pants, and lay on the front verandah in the swing hammock, with the Japanese houseboy sitting beside her, smoking and filling her big tankard with beer. By and by she sat on the steps in a little white sports suit and turned the little skirt up to her waist. Her great bare thighs and legs and feet looked disgusting and the loud talk attracted all the passers-by. What can one do? It's sickening, unclean. Oh, how splendid it will be when there is no more sex. It should be beautiful but we've spoilt it, and it can be loathsome, sex not used for the propagation of the species but for lust.

AUGUST 4TH

I am impossible today so I try to keep by myself. Too mean a bag to mix. Oh, this autumn of years that has already turned to early winter. The worst thing about it is the weary drag of the body. Tired, tired. The work doesn't abate, but the strength does. Beautiful souls can rise above it with souls stronger than flesh. I can't. I [am] just an old earthly being. I do long for that rising quality, that yeast of spunk that won't be drowned by aches. I'm just dough with no rising (unleavened bread), and when very heavy, this and that person blows drafts of cold on you and the dough sinks yet heavier. Then I just detest the entire world, I want to snap and yap like a mean chained pup. I don't care if my teeth and claws are sharp. I'm glad. I want to be left alone and go in my kennel and sulk because everyone's unreliable and mean and does you up and kicks you down. Joy doesn't exist and everything [is] covered with dirt. Why can't people be decent? This disgusting business of tumbling in and out of marriage. I'm not for squabbling couples. Life's too short, and if there's a reason, I say divorce. Drinking, women, or cruelty or beastliness I would not stand [for], but just to flop out of one pair of arms into another without even a good fight to warrant it like B and F disgusts me. It has all been a sort of a blow, a tumbling down of ideals and idols. I don't feel any more interest in them and their philosophy of life, but there's a blank space on the wall where the door was not only shut but plastered over and made into a solid wall. No door to even unlock sometimes and peep in. I wonder if they will ever write to me. I doubt [it]. They are all wrapped up in their new mates and have no interest outside. Long alone, I became a boring nonentity to them in art. Then an active opposition in religion. There is not a thing left to bind. We're like parsnip roots growing.

AUGUST 12TH

I haven't one friend of my own age and generation. I wish I had. I don't know if it's my own fault. I haven't a single thing in common *with them. They're all snarled up in grandchildren or W.A. or church teas or bridge or society. None of them like painting and they particularly dislike my kind of painting. [...]* A lunatic, a prostitute and a Chinese artist — these are among my friends. I have rewritten the "Throat and a Monkey's Hands." Tried to get some construction, suspense and climax in it. It's great fun. I *want* to make the thing hang together, make the creatures real and *make* people love them.

AUGUST 15TH

Heaven forgive me. How I hate tenants. Always trying to squeeze something out of you, always trying to make out they're being done in or not getting their pound of flesh, always finding shortcomings in you and your house. Snivelling, whining, squeezing, hypocritical vermin. Susie the rat is a lady compared to most of 'em. Bristles burst out of every crevice of my vertebrae and I long to do one of Woo's faces at them. Alice sits there and lets those cheap English tramp all over her. I spit like a cat at every tap of their beastly heels. I detest that type. Those cheap, bragging, swanking English are rennet wine to my life's milk. They sour and curdle me. Lie down, oh flesh. Get up, spirit. Hoist me above the miring clay.

I've had old Mrs. Rollins today. Eighty-two. Shall I be like that twenty years from now? *No*, I shan't be nearly so nice or sweet. It's too bad for folks to live alone. I feel and know it. You centre too much round yourself. She wasn't tethered to her ego.

SEPTEMBER 9TH

[...] Written to Lawren just as if they were like they used to be. I wonder what Bess has done to him. Has she helped or hindered his work? None of my business.

OCTOBER 5TH

[...] Alice phoned and said great niece Betty B. was at the house with her mother and her baby, and I'd better come down. I had not seen Betty for years, not since she grew up. She's very tall and bright and happy and proud of her baby. She kissed me. Una, her mother, sat by Alice's fire. They all sat round it, even Campbell who doesn't belong was there. When I went in the music stopped and there was no chair for me. I bowed to Una and said good evening and a horrible feeling ran round the circle. I knew I must not stay. I went down to the bedroom and saw the child (my great grandnephew) and talked a few minutes to Betty and called the pups and came away home again to the big empty lonesome house. Oh why? Eleven years ago Una said those bitter things. Even as she wrote them she did not know if I was already dead. I was undergoing a bad operation and she wrote that it was to be hoped I would die and not live to be a burden and a nuisance to the others. Why should her "dear Aunt Bet" be burdened with a hateful crosspatch to wait on? She supposed the trouble I was

being operated on for was one reason I'd been such a hateful crank all my life, etc. etc. Lizzie left the letter lying on my desk. It was addressed to Miss Carr, 646 Simcoe Street. It began "Dear Auntie" and was in my blotter. I read it thinking it was for me. Soon I saw but read on, stung to the quick. Una and I had never hit it off. We were too near of an age for aunt and niece. She was beautiful—I stupid—I was gifted but ordinary. I suppose that beast jealousy poked in. Well, I wrote to her and said I *was dead to her.* I did not meet her for over ten years. Lizzie and Alice adore her and count it all my fault. Is it? If any one wishes you dead, why live to them? Best be dead. I wish her no ill, I just want to leave her alone and forget her. Breaks like that don't mend. Of course, Lizzie sides entirely with her and condemns my wickedness. If the Devil himself was pitted against me, she'd side with him. It has always been so. She is good to me because she is good and likes to do her duty. But she condemns me always; in all I do or say, she is on the other side. Oh God, why do you fix families so? Why make a nice family and then chuck in a misfit? Mother knew and she was the only being who ever did. She knew I was her ugly duck. When Dede would try and break my will and got mad because she couldn't, that was what she hurled—Mother's worry at leaving me because I was wayward and different to her other children. If we reincarnate again as children, oh I do hope I'll belong and not be a sort of patch stuck on after the family's made. If I've ever grumbled at the lonesomeness, they've said it's because I'm selfish or something. Both their lives are cram full of souls. I don't want a lot, but oh just a few right ones.

The downstairs folk had visitors today. I saw them come. Mr. and Mrs. dashed out onto the pavement and hugged and kissed them as they got out of the motor. Such genuine delight and hubbub and happy talk and arms circling and tongues wagging. They left the blinds up a little tonight and all sat around the fire in good fellowship. Even the Jew next door has his ladies-in-the-sun. He is a bachelor but never alone in his home.

This being cast alone must be to teach me something. Sometimes I wonder if it was that ungovernable love that possessed me for so many years pouring out, pouring out wasted and unwanted 'til, ill and worn with the canker of it, I wrenched it out of my being and trampled on it. Threw it from me and grew cold and hard and dead. By and by the roots sprouted again and wanted to grow but there wasn't any good earth for them to grow in. It was all built over in brick and stone and pavement. The poor little roots tried to get a hold but couldn't. And strong winds blew (as it were) a little dust among the roots to keep them just alive, and the dust is the love of the blessed creatures, monkey and dogs and blessed little rat offering the rootlets of my love nourishment and shelter.

OCTOBER 14TH

Life was completely beastly. I turned the Sunday *Colonist* with its noxious fumes of death and destruction pouring from every page and looked out at the high blue sky and autumning foliage. No peace on earth, no goodwill towards men. My own heart was bitter towards many.

OCTOBER 29TH

Will she go tomorrow? I told her to, gave her a month's notice and a reminder in the month's middle. It's horrid living over top of a woman like that. She wants everything and to pay for nothing. She wants to impress me with her importance. She brags of her breeding but she has none — not even as much as an earwig. It says in the insect book earwigs are quite noble. They brood their young, not to hatch them with their warmth but to protect them against enemies. She's beastly to her child. He's coarse and rude because she doesn't teach him. She resents him because she must support him. In the morning you hear her smack, smack, and he roar, roar. At half past eight the child stumps coarsely down the pavement. He is only three. His arms thrust themselves into the sleeves of his homemade jacket. No mother's hand adjusting, pulling the cuff of his jersey down, adjusting the shoulder and tweaking the tail like real mothers do. He is fed, spanked and sent. I'd hate to be her child. "I am a widow," she moaned, trying to jew down the prices when she came. "A widow with child."

OCTOBER 30TH

Oh me. Oh dearie dearie me. Sore and trembling all over. Worse with the conflict and hatefulness. It was just dreadful. Her month was up yesterday but she did not get out. This morn I said (left a note under the door) that another month's rent began today unless her things were removed, for I'd a notion she wanted her half day, Saturday, and so I could have allowed her if she'd been decent and the rent paid. The van came and I told the man her rent must be paid before her things went. She rushed out in a passion, hurling insults etc. I kept on saying, "Be still, be still," but stayed firm. Then I phoned the police and they told me to keep back stuff. I went to the bin at the back and took the garbage can — the only useful and decent thing in her little flat — and was making off with the clothes basket full of rubbish when she tore upstairs after me, seized it and began shaking me

in a passion. "Give my things back," she shrieked. I told her I had
the police authority. All I wanted was the rent. I did not want
her things. I took the old bucket on top and slipped it over her
head, saying, "Take them then. The police will come. I shall
leave it to them." She did look foolish struggling with the basket
and bucket on her head and the screams pouring from under
it. "I'll smash everything in the house," she thundered. So I
phoned, the police sent out a big, strong man and advised her
not to. Then he told me to pick anything to the value of what
she owed. "I don't want anything she's got, I only want my rent."
However, he suggested a standing lamp, a poor wooden thing,
and I said, "I have her garbage can." With that, she flew into a
fearful spasm of rage and vituperation. "And I want my keys," I
said. He made her hand them over, front and back door. She said
she wouldn't give them up 'til she was ready, but he made her
and told me to take the lamp away and lock it up. Well, I will
strive to forget her as hard as I can. Clean up her dirt and be
thankful to be rid of the creature.

They have just left. I was in the front and she turned like a
fool and kissed her hand to me about six times grinning like
a maniac. I wonder if she is crazy.

NOVEMBER [3RD?]
Alice shakes her head and says, "I wish you had not." I did not
hurt the reptile and it *was* fun. If my sister had done that, I'd
have loved her for it and not said, "I wish you had not." I'm
always sympathetic and sorry when people do their means. I've
tried dutifully hard to do right by that awful white woman and
I do think that there are limits to what one should allow in
their houses. If one gets just a little bit...

NOVEMBER 9TH

[...] Been forlorn in heart all day and can't say why. The big house
seems so empty, *is* so empty. Space talks, so all those empty rooms
keep up the chatter every time you pass them, reminding you
they are empty, and all the "feels" of all the people who were ever
in them float round, in and out of the doors and windows of them.
People always leave "feels" in a place they occupy—live, eat,
think in. It ought to make one mighty careful. What thoughts go
on like that, what ones they entertain. Yesterday I was hanging
clothes on the drying rack and such a commotion around my
feet. I called Pout and Tantrum to order severely, for they'd just
come in from the garden and I did think they could have worked
their beans off there. But when I looked, it was Wopper, Wop who
I gave away five or six weeks ago and the woman "lost." It took
her all that while to find me again. She went off in a motor and
she never went on the street and didn't know her way about and
it was miles off she went, but she came back Thursday, rough
and poor in coat, ravenous, eczemic, lame in one leg, dull eyed and
desperately tired and hungry. When I saw it was Wop, I gave her
a great hunk of birthday cake (Lizzie's) and joy! We rejoiced. The
dog has known suffering in that five weeks. I bathed her and fixed
up the eczema and fed her and got the travelling coop with clean
bedding, and she crept in and slept and rested all day, dog tired all
right. She did not even want to come when I took the others out,
just seemed as if she'd found her place. So sad yet content to be
home. Gee, what love and fidelity. A nervous shy little dog at the
mercy of anybody's kick, living on any garbage she could rustle,
out in the cold and wet and wind, sleeping where she could. She
must have gone miles, yet always remembering. I shall never part
with her again. She's back for life and she knows it.

In the middle of last night, I lay hearing creaks and rattles present beside me in bed. A soft little "creepy furry" up against me close. Now, why sit up like a fool and flip it across the bed with a startled hand, even if it had been a mouse? But I did, and before my hand had completed the flip, I knew it was Susie the white rat [who] crept up in the still black of the night just to see her beloved was sleeping. Soon as the realization came to me, I took the little soft warm thing and cuddled her up. Loving little white Susie. She was truly very triumphant and gay, and what a joy it is for the creatures to find one down on their level. She went round and round my neck, tried to make a nest in my hair, licked my face and crept into my palms for little spells. Then I dropped off to be roused by Susie squirming between my palms for it was night and not her sleeping time. She'd done that all day, now she was for investigation. I was afraid of turning in my sleep and crushing her so I got up and took her down to the studio, and tonight I shut the door. But I love Susie. Our two "reals" meeting. Nothing to do with white fur and pink skin and ticking red heart pumps but the tickle of life that is in us.

NOVEMBER 14TH

[...] The lost dog's eyes change every day. Less of the dulled, weary, frightened torment remains. She loves to have a bandage put on her lame leg. It makes her feel important and cared for, apart from, partly, the ease of support. She cannot bear to have me out of sight. She is throwing out little tendrils like a creeping vine and thrusting them through my cracks so it will be impossible to shift her off to another body because she's mine, and to tear her off, I'd tear myself. So there we are. Too many dogs for one house, but not too many for one heart.

NOVEMBER 17TH

[...] I went to have my new coat fitted. Charlie Wo, a Chinese tailor, is making it. The shop is dark as a rat hole. Old Charlie Wo and Mrs. Charlie Wo and Miss Charlie Wo swarmed into the tiny shop, crusted with pins and tape and buttons and chalk, and Mr. Charlie Wo did things with chewing gum, pins and string, but no one paid any attention to him. I stood under a dim light and looked into a dim mirror up pretty near the ceiling, and the Wo family all talked together in Chinese over me. Then one would jab a pin in some part of me and both the others would screech. Pa was boss, Ma had more sense, and daughter most English. When I made a suggestion, the girl told Ma, Ma told Pa, then Pa responded to Ma, who responded to the girl, who retold the information to me. Quite some job getting a fitting.

NOVEMBER 18TH

A happy day. Harry Adaskin of the Hart House Quartet came to lunch and we talked more than we ate. [...] I feel lots better about Lawren and Bess. His view of it is big and broad and fine and made me feel ashamed, for the whole affair had cut and seared. I shall write them now, I think. Before, I did not seem to know what to say.

NOVEMBER 26TH

[...] I went to the Empire Theatre to hear Clem Davis on the Second Coming of Christ this morning. And I went to the same place with Lee Nan, the Chinaman, to see a Chinese movie talkie last Wednesday. There you are! Life's a mix. I suppose my every experience on earth is an ingredient, some substantial and some only flavourings that scarcely show, but the beating

of them all together will make one compounded article. God has the receipt. We can only guess how much of each ingredient should go in, and according as we add more of this or that, will our cake be good or bad.

DECEMBER 5TH

I heard a real love story last night. Sex and materiality left out. Big, wide, unselfish love, very beautiful, a love outside of our word "love."

DECEMBER 8TH

I am going to put it into words made of letters. Our mind clambers round the forming of the symbols of speech. Maybe the formed letters catch something the ear misses, or by forming the crude symbols, the mind finds out through the eye a little more of the meaning. This thing has been between us all our lives, seems like, without reason on her side or mine. The cat in her and the cat in me spit at each other. I love her, I admire her, I revere her. What she feels for me, I can't say. I never found the way into her heart to find out. It's such bosh to say another thinks thus and so. How does anybody *know* what anybody else feels inside? It's guesswork entirely. No matter what she *really* thought about me and felt for me, I know from her point of Christianity that she'd have to love me as a part of her Christian duty. I've been tempted many times to feel her love for me ended right there. When I am sick, she is kind to me — she is to everyone. She loves to dominate the sick and would go to the limits of unselfish attention for "sick duty." When I am well, she treats me as a fool, an outcast from her point of view, to her ideas of Christianity. I do not attend her church. Other churches are only back and side doors of Heaven. Hers leads smack up to the gold front stairs and are the only totally respectable ones. She never gives me credit for decent feelings in anything, contests all I say, sides with the opposing party every time against me, says I'm hateful, always hateful, says I'm stupid, clicks her tongue and shakes her head continuously at my stupidity because I am deaf and has no patience and no sympathy, sides with anyone who gives me a kick, jeers at my tastes, outlook, abilities etc. Now why??? Has she reason??? Am I that thing she thinks is me at all? Is there no good thing in me at all? Am I utterly selfish, utterly stupid, utterly hateful, utterly mean? Oh Lord. I do not feel concerted by her opinions of me and I spit back, that horrid cat in me humps and hisses, because no matter how loving and kind you may feel when you go in, she always sticks darts in you and twists them and riles those things you never meant to come out, and [you] go out the door on the run before you say more because you do not want to quarrel with her. I love her and she's sick. She's the first person I ever remember quarrelling with. She loved Alice deeply. So did I. Alice was the halfway between us two. When she bickered too hard, I kicked over the traces. She knew exactly how to aggravate. Then, when you threw all sanity and reason to the winds and hit and tore and scratched, she put on the saint and quoted scripture. Oh why, oh why, oh why, oh why?

There I go; back to *kind, generous, lovely* things she has done for me and call myself a beast and a snake. Sometimes it was hard to accept things because they were so seasoned with sharpness and hatefulness, but you really loved her too much to hurt her by refusing and you took them and felt like a sewer for lowness. I remember [when I was] a baby I bit her arm. Mother tied me up to the verandah. It was dark, and she tied me with a strip of soft flannel, put the dog pan down, told me to bite anything that came and shut the door. I was terrified of dark. It was dreadful. I could hear them just the other side of the kitchen door. Chops were sizzling for supper, I remember the smell. Another time I scratched her hand. I can feel the burning shame now at those two or three nail marks on the back of her hand. How vile I was and yet how supremely she could aggravate and go off with that saintly air and a test thrown back at you. How she knew just how to set the match that burnt you with flame. Poor soul, poor dear soul, and she's sick and we can't do a thing to help her, she keeps us so distant and littles up her hurt. Even as I write she came again, kindly solicitous for my indisposition. I really believe she does love me, not like she loves Alice and not for myself but because I'm a "Carr" and family affection is story and claimed. There's an ache of longing after her when she goes. I wonder if she feels it too and why nothing on earth seeming could smash that steel armour of reserve. How would it have been, I wonder, if I'd been born four years first instead of her? I wonder how we'd have felt reversed in ages. Would she have seemed foolish and stupid to me as I looked down those four years? Would I have seemed so wise looking up as she does to me? She has a much clearer mind than mine. I respect her judgement when she gives me the chance and doesn't annihilate me by saying, "You're rubbish."

JANUARY IST, 1935

[...]

> The song is to the singer, and comes back but to him
> The murder is to the murderer, and comes back but to him
> Not one can acquire for another, not one
> Not one can grow for another, not one.
> —Walt Whitman [*Leaves of Grass*]

I hope 1935 will bring me more zest for work, more inspiration. Maybe I'll have to be stripped of everything, even my house, before I come down to brass tacks. God, humanity, my work—if I only could burst forth with live, spontaneous, bursting love like the throbbing love I had for the birds when I was a child and stood tiptoe to peep into a nest. The secret and mystery, the ecstasy of wonder and love that thrilled me to the very core! If one could only feel that all again, and the love you had for Mother when you'd been bad and she'd been patient, a sort of shy and adoring love, so thoroughly comfortable a kind of love. And the love of the lover sweeping you clean off your feet, making you forget the horrible sex things told so disgustingly when you were a little child, things that frightened you horribly. And yet in the passionate love of the lover, forgetting every bit of the horror, willing to give every bit of your body and life and love in floodtide ocean fairly drowning the beloved, and to find it was not wanted and never, never, to quite know why, only to know it must be so, and to eat one's heart out *alone* always, never daring to tell a soul, shamed and broken and hurt at your own indecency, of loving so furiously, so overwhelmingly—unasked and unwanted—to find the caresses and kisses were only sport, selfish amusement, your heart used as a shuttlecock, batted furiously hither and thither only lasting one game, thrown aside, feathers broken, balance broken, a hideous, battered, smashed-up toy that could never be mended or straightened again. Only good for *one* game, then finding its way to the garbage can, grimed and fouled. Oh love, poor love. Not mended or soothed and strengthened but murdered and thrown out and towed far far out to sea and dumped. Oh! Is it possible that it will be washed and purged and buffeted and perchance cleaned by great washings in the sea, will be cast ashore again?

JANUARY 28TH [1935]

Lecture not so bad last night. Good deal of analysis. One can analyse too far and become a machine building mechanically. On the other hand, one can (like me) hustle a thing into being without organization. Then the first kick tumbles it over. Balance and horse sense is what counts. The sickly insincere slop of flattery before and after lectures nauseates me. [...]

FEBRUARY 14TH, VALENTINE'S

It was brought to my mind in the wee hours by Susie. She was my valentine two years ago and while it was yet dark up she came to my bed. Who would believe the love and sweetness that can be wrapped up in a little white rat? In the night like that she is so peppy and so lively, rubbing against my cheek, licking my hands, going through and through the hollow between one's shoulder and one's head on the pillow. Thrusting her head up with little quick jerks and pushing here and there among one's cheeks, among the fingers of your hand and under your chin and begging to have her ears rubbed and her chin. Then she flats down and oozes contentment and satisfaction and gives soft little happy squeakings. In the daytime she seldom leaves the big studio table, though she sticks her nose out of the basket of rags, when I call her, in a drowsy fashion. At night she's quivering with life. If I've been writing, she goes among my papers; if sewing, she flits among my work. Anywhere where the smell of her beloved is fresh. That rat loves me.

Man's effect on woman is queer. Apparently a woman may love another woman genuinely. Let a man come into their life. Phiz! Out goes the other woman; just incidental [to] your friend you were, and their man is the all supreme with them. It hurts. I don't think it would ever be that way with me, if the other woman was close to me. Seems to me women friends are not "stickers." Maybe married ones who have both families and husbands in common are, but spinsters and married women are not. The married woman always feels so superior to the spinster, and you know what you say to her passes to her man. It's best to say goodbye forever when a woman gets a man. One cannot *trust* men. Even if one married I don't believe they could quite, in all the world. I do not know of one I'd trust, and married women the same because of their men.

Life's hideous just now, everyone anxious and pinched and unnatural and sore about something, and some wicked fairy has turned all the blood and flesh hearts into affairs of tin and lead and stone with all the warm soft gone out. Just a hard dry ache and a "hungry want." Where have you gone to, joy? You are ached out of existence.

There is a woman with many children and a husband that drinks. Her lot is very sore. I think I could not bear it, I should be bitter and nasty. I think her love for him is frayed at the edges but she worries for fear of what may happen to him if he comes to calamity driving home drunk. The wonder is what would happen to them all if his salary (a good portion of which goes to the bottle) were totally withdrawn. Does she, can she, still love him for himself? Looking at marrieds, I often wonder how much is love and how much the ordinary needs of life, like when one is in danger of losing their job, being afraid of being without it.

Friendship — what does it mean? None of us knows any of us. It sickens me sometimes. Those close hugs, those kisses and confidences, they don't mean a thing except for a heartbeat or two.

The connection was never fast grown. It broke so easily. This heart went bitter. That heart went; your shoulders shrugged and that was the end. No gum, no bridging, can mend it; the old wound would always show. Maybe lazy fat would collect and hide the injury, but [when] the weather changes, the old injury would grumble and remind you.

[...] Max [Maynard] has just been in. We always disagree a little. I do not think we understand each other. We have different slants on work. Some folks buck you, some leave you like a wilted cabbage, some like a frosted one, so that your unpleasantness reaches out to those near you and you wait to pour ashes on your work and to dance on your hat. He likes my work sometimes, but in an unpleasant way. A way that depresses you.

MARCH

Last night I dreamt of Lawren and Bess, a happy dream. They were married. I was with them and said to myself, "I am so happy I've found them again and the new arrangement hasn't made a difference, only made things better between us." Bess was chattering away, but Lawren said nothing as is always the way. He never speaks in dreams, but he laid his two hands on me and smiled. Poor Lawren. I loved his work and should, but his body—I don't know how to put it. It shivered—repelled me.

Everyone is waiting and waiting and waiting these days and nobody knows for what. There is a lonely blue brooding over everything. Everything is so difficult. People's bodies and hearts are aching. It is not all because people's purses are empty. It's some other dreary, lonesome thing. We're off the boil, no cheerful sing, no quivering lid, just a sullen lukewarmness, sooted on the bottom and furred within. Oh for a jolly old fire to set life's kettle singing and bubbling and steaming!

It's "Doxies" that sharpen the edges of Bess and I against each other. She is "author" and I "unauthor," the Doxies that becomes one hideousifies the other. Life, dress, food, recreation, work, companions. Tasks, furniture, houses, gardens, looks, books, friends, churches, religion. She looks one way, I another. I suppose if we both looked straight out ahead we'd be OK and maybe that's what Heaven will really be — everyone seeing things straight, looking neither right or left but straight out in front, and the straight front look will be so broad and clean and right that the crooked side way will be forgotten. There won't be any "Doxies" at all. Neither "author" nor "unauthor" but just one grand broad rightness — beautiful! No one will want to say, "I told you so," because it won't be to the right or the left like either of us thought but plumb ahead, and we'll both want to step in line with a delighted chortle of joy and no venom. [...]

SPRING AND SUMMER
1935

APRIL 3RD

[...] There is something comforting about writing, sort of explaining things to yourself. When I was frustrated, I thought of other people; I connected what they would think with what I wrote. It's different now. It's sort of easier for wondering. One talks to so few people, and so few out of these few understand each other; some make you feel a dreadful fool. Other times they're the fool and you're the important one.

Today and tomorrow it will be my sketches on exhibition and I shall hate it because it expresses me more. The old Indian pictures expressed the Indians. There was only an insignificant splatter of me. They made the cake and I only had to cut it and hand it around. Any fool could do that. With these, they'll want the receipt and what the cookbook calls "method of procedure," and I don't use a cookbook. I throw in to taste, overseasoning, underseasoning, burning, omitting "raisins," having "doughy" results. When people ask you to explain a painting, how can one? Do you have to explain why the cat yowls if you step on her tail?

APRIL 4TH

Not so many came as to the Indian pictures but quite a few all the same. And many who had been to the Indian exhibition came again, which showed they were interested enough in the painting side to see what was happening next. It was interesting to see their reaction to the two types. About the Indian things they talked more and their remarks [were] more superficial. They discussed Indian ways and the disappearing race, but mostly the money value of things when they had ceased to exist. To the sketches, their attitude was quite different. They looked much, thought much and said little. Money value was not discussed, but they were interested (some of them) deeply. You felt something stirring around the rooms. They took the Indians "sitting." Nobody sat to the sketches. They moved, went back and forth, were more awake and alive. Something seemed to be waking up inside them, something that slept gently through the Indian exhibit. Gee, I'd like to wake myself sufficiently to run and set the sitters and the standers into a gallop.

APRIL 8TH

How tired one can get and not die! When the exhibition closed yester-day I longed to get to painting. First, however, the flat the exhibition was in had to be got ready for a tenant. The kitchen was peeling. I bolted out of bed this morning right on to the stepladder with a knife and those walls had to be scraped inch by inch. I did not give myself time to think. I said, "Put your whole zest into that, old girl. It's nec-essary, so make it worth while. When it is all clean maybe you can paint." Life is such a continual struggle inside. The desire to hurl yourself entirely into paint, line up in another world where apartment houses, family relations, gardens, tenants, friends, clothes, food do not exist. And combatting all that innate desire to "do all things decently and in order" to have a clean decent home, to love my sisters and do my duty to them, to help in their lives, for if I did not go to them, they would so rarely come to me we should almost be strangers.

Everything in life seems to contradict something else. If I was a real artist I'd let everything else go, but I can't and don't and so I'm not. [...]

APRIL IITH

[...] Oh the awful constant wrestle between this and that. It is not so hard to measure up to justice. One's instincts lead to that, but to heap mercy on top of justice without being unfair to one-self, that is difficult. In dealing with tenants now, if you will let them, they take every advantage of you they can. If they cannot get it by fair means, they'll take it out by unfair. My whole soul cries out against the letting business. People are poor these days,

but oh they are selfish, forgetting that owners are poor too with the grinding taxes, constant repairs, vacancies. They hound and jew one. You are always only the darned landlady, a little juice to get the best of. That's where mercy and softness get tangled. I've tried my level [best] to be decent to those tenants; under our contract they were to give work in return for all the "gratis" I [have] thrown in (all the furniture) and $5 off rent. The woman declared any of them would do anything for me. For the past year it has been only wood, and that done as a favour. Four healthy adults have sat in that flat and heard and seen me labour like a char, with folded hands they've sat without an offer of help.

There is another battle constantly waging inside me. Artist and domestic. Trying to be honest to both wears one sharp. The last six months have been almost all plain domestic. My soul is thirsty.

APRIL 14TH

[...] Goodbye little white rat Susie. I found her halfway across the studio floor headed for my bedroom but dead, this morning. She had outlived her span of life and it had become to her a burden, and I tucked her away in the good brown earth under the lilac tree, glad her wearinesses were over. It is astonishing the empty feel of the big table where she lived. I always spoke to her as I passed, and there was always that companionable little nip of her life came out and met you with ready response. She had a free happy life and I loved her well.

APRIL 21ST — EASTER DAY

[...] Went to eight o'clock celebrations at the cathedral. Church full. I met them coming from the seven o'clock. I wonder why people look so very self-conscious and smug when they are going and coming from Communion, especially in the early morning? They clutch their prayer books and give you a sort of "you" look, much as to say, "Did not know you were that sort." I often wonder what they are praying about so long there upon their knees yet vividly alert to what is going on around them. And those who go seldom and are not at home and have to peep to see what the ones in front are doing. I am afraid I do not follow the sermon much from my book. I cannot hear so I shut my eyes and just try to feel Christ, and to feel all the thoughts that have tried to struggle up to him there.

I think the most impressive moment of all is when after the little pause the clergyman says, "The peace of God which passeth all understanding keep your hearts and minds." As a very tiny girl, those words always slipped something inside me. Something seemed to pass through the church, and then we got up and came out and the porch chatter began.

Clem Davies had a dawn service at Mount Tolmie, illuminated cross, piano accordion music, special streetcars and buses and whole paraphernalia of movie pictures, I suppose to break the solemnity, shoving their cameras through the crowd during prayers. It rained hard in the night so everyone would have cold wet feet and before they had time to rise above the wet feet and the cameramen, the prayers would be done. All the same it may mean a whole lot to many people. We don't all want the same food cooked the same way. It's what we can digest nourishes us. I wish I could worship with the unselfconsciousness of a dog absorbing the sunshine, without comment but with complete content, letting the warmth of it course right through his body unconsciously.

Everyone loves the griffons—these three are cute and friendly. They are "persons" of character with attractions added. But what a dog Koko was. What a heart so staunch and true. I wonder where he is now and the other faithful loving things I've had. Every creature I ever possessed had given so lavishly of its best, not keeping anything back, returning the love I gave over and over, adding interest and handing back an amazing sum. What becomes of all that accumulation? It can't dissolve, fade away. Somehow, somehow, it's a concrete thing building up—part of God's endless plan that grows and grows and never gets stale or old but reaches out wider and higher and deeper.

APRIL 22ND—EASTER MONDAY

[...] For the second time we three met at Lizzie's and after supper read from Father's diary. That diary has given me a whole new slant on Father. Coming near the end of a big family, I only knew a cross, gouty, sexy old man who hurt and disgusted me. I resented his omnipotence and his selfishness and I was frightened of him. He knew he had hurt and frightened me, telling me things a happy innocent child should not hear and telling them in a low and blatant manner. When he saw the horror he had created in me he was bitter, probably more with himself than me. Then he was cruel and I hated him. I can feel the awful relief still when I stood by his grave and it was being filled up. Thud, thud, the clods fell on the box. They had closed the lid of the box shell with a clap. It sounded deep and hollow down in the open grave. We all stood around in deep black mourning. I was closest. I was peering down into the fast filling hole and in my heart there was *relief*. Nobody knew the sinking agonies of terror I had suffered when I had been alone with Father, because before I'd been his favourite trotting after him like a dog. Now I was free, the first time for several years. The old family doctor came up and put his arms around me. "Come lassie," he said, "this is no place for you." But none of them knew, not one, what feelings were going on in me. I couldn't forgive Father, I just couldn't, for spoiling all the loveliness of life with that bestial brutalness of an explanation, filling me with horror instead of gently explaining the glorious beauty of reproduction, the holiness of it. Mother died two years before, it happened before [she died], but I never told her. I was too shy. How she would have grieved; perhaps she knew more than I thought. I have seen her look perplexed and worried when I begged not to have to go and meet Father in the evenings after business as had been my custom. Poor little Mother. Her life must have had some sad spots. I am sure Father loved her, but he loved himself more.

Now from this old diary of Father's I can see he must have been a fine young man: strong and brave, honest and kindly and energetic. Plenty of perseverance and plenty of pluck. He seemed fond of his parents too. His experiences and impressions of the New World are most interesting, but he remained an Ultra English Englishman 'til he died. His heart was more than British, it belonged to England itself. [...]

MAY 9TH

[...] Life gets more and more difficult, and dying seems to get harder and harder. No more gently turning a face to the wall and gently flitting from the flesh. Either people die a violent death or they seem to have one long awful battle at the end. So the new medicine methods make it easier — or harder — by taking drugs and undergoing operations. The torture is prolonged. What does it mean, God? To suicide is hideously sinful, [but] is it by chance God giving them a final chance to prove their bravery?

Clem Davies says angels are graduate souls and all of us have one or more special angels near and helping us on in spiritual [ways], enough so we could feel their presence and take comfort in them.

MAY 29TH

When comfortably sleepy, you climb into a comfortable bed, hump your knees, plunk your soles on a red-hot water bottle, pile the pillows high at your back, put a little woollie round your shoulders and your specs on your nose and your book on your knees. There really seems little else to be desired, 'specially if you have one of those toffee blobs on a stick known as an all-day-sucker to lick at and you have not done or said anything particularly beastly that day. So you can contentedly read a little, pray a little, sleep and perhaps dream some "splendid" halfpenny or go to some interesting place where the most incongruous things seem perfectly natural. In dreams the delight is that there is no sex, no size, no foolishness; you perform the most astounding feats without effort. You get without going, see without eyes and laugh without a mouth. You encounter people you've never seen and meet people you have. Everything is topsy-turvy yet more completely "right" than this world ever thought of being, so that when you are starting to wake you keep pushing yourself back again, hating to come into ordinariness again.

Dreams can hurt hard. I went, in the dream, to the station to meet Bess. She had returned my greeting in a cold abstract way, seeming in a violent hurry as if she had a train to connect with or someone to meet. She flashed up a stair and was gone.

It was my place, my town — sore, I wandered round the hotel a primitive affair with doors opening onto balconies. Looking up, I saw Bess dressing in a room. She came out onto the balcony with Tantrum and began pouring coal oil on him, rubbing it in. Oh, I thought, she did not even tell me she had Tantrum and she knew I loved him and would want to see him. It seemed she had got him from me in the East and I longed to see the little dog and touch him. And there through the open door I saw a wicker chair and over the back was Lawren's suit and hat. So he was there too and had not even come to speak to me. They were done with me and excluding me. I turned away sore.

Dreams are foolish. It does not do to set store by them. Friendship? What is that but misunderstanding and disappointment?

JULY 4TH

[...] Garland Anderson, negro playwright, philosopher and psychologist took the pulpit today. He spoke on the personality of Jesus. Jesus said, "Follow me," not "Worship me." He spoke with magical interpretation, a good bit. For example, a composer was in San Francisco and heard a player play his composition. The player did not know he was the composer. The composer asked him to play the thing again. "Thank you," he said at the finish, "I wrote that. I did not know it was so beautiful; your interpretation added much to my thought." So — to get a great piece of music, it must be gone over and over faithfully, each one adding to its beauty as it passes along, something worth while (if he has something worth while in himself) 'til the thing is beautiful and perfected. I thought much the same applied to painting. Some man has an idea; others build and build, adding riches to it.

We as selfish hearts wish to keep it *our own*. It is not. Nothing is ours. We are only permitted to play with the building blocks.

JULY 16TH

Went to hear Garland Anderson at the Empress Hotel. It is the same thing, nothing new. If one could only grasp it, this terrible doubting. How does one overcome that? One wants it above all (they think they do). Then they drift back and close up again and sleep and drift. The process of waking is very slow. The big hall was full, everybody wanting, longing for something; a thirsty lot but afraid to drink. Like when you come to a stream in the woods with thick growth to the water's edge and you are afraid to let your feet down amongst it for fear of snakes and mud and wasps' nests. But the tinkle of the water is so tantalizing and the shine of it through the long branches; and the first leg that goes down between the logs and branches gets the skin scraped and you squeal, pull it back and wish someone would reach out and hand it back to you in a cup. And if they did, it wouldn't taste half so good as if you lay flat on a tippy log and lapped it for yourself.

Anderson started out, "Delight thyself in the Lord." How marvellous to feel that ecstasy and delight. How can one? There we stand shivering at the dark underneaths of the growth instead of plunging and risking and reaching our drink, in spite of slime and wasps and snakes. Gee! We are a slumpy lot.

He spoke about "heart's desire" and our desire being God's desire for us. Suppose a man desired another man's wife? What the man really desired was the love and joy that particular connection would bring him. God might grant his prayer but in another way, giving him his desire but not the other man's wife. So in praying for anything, think of the spiritual side, its bigger realization, the essence of the desire, not its material form. In answer to a question about the selling of real estate: know that somewhere what you have would be useful and acceptable to someone. Pray that the Father will bring that one to what he wants and that you may both, by the just and fair exchange, be satisfied. Want to give [to] the other man as well as to get yourself.

Use the God power within us We are greater than our minds or wills because God power is within us. It is given to us to use. Christ used it and came to show us how to do so. Jesus did not think it wrong to use good things. The wine at the wedding was a luxury, not a necessity. He did not say to the people, "You are spiritual, you do not need wine," or to the multitudes, "You are spiritual, you do not need food." He produced it When the tax money was due, he produced it from the fish's mouth. He rendered unto Caesar the things that were Caesar's and to God the things that were God's. [...] In our minds are many thoughts. Among them will be one that will supply our need. It may not be our own selection. We think of our business, our house, our job as the only means of livelihood, but if we cast about among our thoughts we shall find as he found the fish.

JULY 17TH

Last night, Garland Anderson lecture. The hall was filled and interest keen. There were many questions answered at the end. "Do you believe in reincarnation?" "I accept it. It seems the logical thing but I do not know any more than anyone else." Some people asked foolish questions about wives or husbands. He was courteous, dignified and kind, but he did not stoop to foolery. Gee, how grand to live in the consciousness and attitude that he does, to rely solely on God to understand. He likened God to a great white light. He said that God was in us. We could have as much of God as we contacted and called forth. God did not impose himself on us, He gave us free choice, individuality. He only wanted for us to accept Him.

He said every question had its answer within us. The fact of our asking a question showed there was an answer. God—the God in us—put the question and God answered it. He spoke about trying too hard, using the mentality but holding ourselves open and quiet for God's guidance. That God-given power is in us, was there waiting use. Jesus said, "Of myself, I can do nothing. The Father within me, He doeth the work." Everyone can be that which they wish to become because God is in them, and if we use His power, it never fails. Delight thyself in the Lord and He shall give thee the desire of thy heart.

JULY 18TH

Garland Anderson's subject was sense that was not common— uncommon sense he defined as that we know in our hearts, though maybe we could not prove it mathematically. Long ago common sense said wood floated and iron sank; to say that iron could float would have been called nonsense. By and by, when they discovered displacement and built steel ships that floated, nonsense turned to common sense. Everything was first a thought. The fact of the thought coming showed there was the answer behind it. Things that come to us by intuition are often uncommon sense. Common sense is of the intellect but uncommon sense works in the heart.

Later in the questions he was asked the difference between believing and knowing. You can know lots of things but 'til you believe them in your heart they are not true to you. The whole business is trusting, having faith in the God-given wisdom which is within yourself, being conscious of it so that it can be used by you. In answer to a question about crucifixion, he said the resurrection was far greater to him than the crucifixion. All the teaching in the world would not have proved that to us, only the resurrection after the crucifixion could do that. Asked about little petty troubles and frets, he said, "I look out and see a whole glorious landscape, space, sunshine, sea, land. If a little dog runs across the foreground and I occupy myself with it, allowing it to keep my attention, then my mind is off the big glorious scene and follows the little dog instead."

If one looks beyond the little cares and frets, they see the big glory instead. Asked if ever he had doubts and fears himself, he said, "Surely I do. One cannot prevent their coming but one need not entertain them when they arrive. In wanting to obtain anything, to draw it to yourself, do not busy yourself with thoughts of what you can get, but think first of what you can give. Remember always that God has means of working that we do not know of. Don't tell God how to do a thing, just trust that His wisdom which is in you will show you the thing to do."

I am taking the classes. My sisters gasped when I told them $5! What is $5 if only one can find the practical usage of these things in life? Gradually this thing has worked upon me for many years. Harry Gage's course, Miss Killens, Mr. Weston and now Garland Anderson. These people are all demonstrating what they teach; everyone's method is a little different, but at bottom is the same God idea. We are allowed a choice of methods. Some suit one, some another. Our needs are as different as our temperaments. If God had meant us all to think alike he would not have varied our ingredients so.

I am happy and expectant re classes. Then sudden little rushes of alarm about the money, yet if it meant nothing (money) to me, would it seem so desirable? It's my sisters, I hate to see them struggling on such short means. Do they feel, "Here she is rushing off to another course. What good have the others done her?" But all souls must stand "alone," think things out inside themselves. Lizzie and Alice are both so good, helping this one and that, being so unselfish, so generous. It makes one feel like a grub. I cannot run round the way they do. I'm fat and flabby and get so tired I can't even think. I do not feel as if it was my job. I feel they do too much and get imposed on and then I feel a selfish beast for thinking it. Does God want us always to be meddling round cosseting someone? Sympathy? Yes, but feeding their grunts and selfishness so one never has the time to think or grow or fill out. It's all a horrible muddle. Hard to know when to run and when to sit. Perhaps I'm a beastly sitter.

My house is up, advertised and listed with agents. I am trying to keep neutral, desiring neither way but knowing that God has ways we know not of and that I shall be provided for.

Garland Anderson says he looks on "law" and Lord as synonymous. They are both perfect and unattainable. You can't alter perfection to make it more perfect. The workings of great laws — life, growth, electricity, gravity — are unattainable. They are God's laws. There were a great many questions; his answers are spontaneous, instantaneous. He does not think them out in his own mind but relies solely on the wisdom of God to answer them through his tongue.

I have difficulty realizing God *within me.* It seems presumptuous. Yet Christ said the kingdom of God is within, and there is the statement "Ye are gods." I suppose I have always looked outside, up among the clouds, to God. As [an] illustration of the working of the great laws of nature, he told of cameramen photographing hatching eggs. The chicks were ready to hatch, the camera was ready. They wanted to get the exact moment of hatching. There was a cheep, the camera clicked, and instantly the chipping stopped. Nature, the law of God, told the chick, warned it. Every time the camera went click, the chick stopped pecking.

Again, he used the chick in reference to Death. He imagined the eggs all there in the nest and the unhatched chicks communicating with each other, wanting to be hatched. Presently one bursts its shell and is free. The others say, "Ho, the chick has gone, he is dead. He is not here among us any more in his shell." He is there but in a different state, and the others can't see him because they have not burst their shells. They are in a different state of consciousness.

My question was — why did Jesus dying voluntarily by his own desire on the cross cry out, "If it be possible, let this cup pass from me"? The answer was — how gloriously it showed Christ's human side. For a moment it transcended, being almost more than he could bear, could go through; then immediately he drew from his divine source and said nevertheless, "Not my way but Thine be done."

Garland Anderson said "I have no illumination." I have seen nothing unnatural or mystic, yet surely he has light within. His outlook is very practical. Practically spiritual, no fancy work.

JULY 19TH

First of G.A's class lessons. The $5.00 course for those who were deeply interested. Questioned about why he should charge for "spiritual readings," he replied, "What one does not pay for they do not value," and it is absolutely true. Have I not proved this in selling puppies? The pup that had no home at all is left to run the streets, and looked upon as a valueless creature as is the gift pup. When it takes a big effort to collect the money, when you have to deny yourself something, then the thing becomes valued. There was a big class. He was painstaking in his explanations. [...]

Your memory is perfect. All events of your life are impressed on the subconscious from cradle to grave. How people will sharply remember unpleasantness down to minute detail and forget the good one after. Memory is perfect. Recollection is what we go wrong in. Remedy for memory: lean on the wisdom of God. [...]

Fear is lack of faith. We have more faith in our fear than in God. Forget what you should forget, elemental fear, uproot negative thoughts. Fear is the root of all negative thinking. Fear is always inverted faith under all conditions.

A child resists pain, is fearful when it sees the cut and the blood, because it does not understand the sharp prick of the mending tissues. Doctors cannot heal and mend, they can help and prepare the way by keeping clean etc., but of themselves they cannot do the work of nature. The adult understands that nature is mending his wound and ceases to fear the little cut. Fear is our creating. The Creator is greater than the thing created, therefore we can master our fear. Plant your faith in what you want, do not try to overcome fear. Overcoming depends on our state of mind, not on learning or understanding but on the power of God within us. [...] Worry is direct effort of faith to have trust. We can always tell when we are trusting by our freeness from worry.

Affirmation: I acknowledge that the power and wisdom of God within me can and will express through me in my fulfilment of desires for success, happiness, needs (painting) etc. The way is an open channel because He knows. The pure spirit of God within me causes me to be aware of its presence.

Five o'clock the day after the last of Garland Anderson's class. All day I have wanted to get to my notes and sit down to face things again, straight and alone. That's the only way. (Alone.)

I started to tell a person who asked if I enjoyed the classes. I made a small futile effort. All the glorious stream I had been flowing with petered out, ending in a ditch, and I wallowing up it without enough water and sticking in the muddy bottom. Now I don't mean the glorious stream wasn't flowing just as ever, the stream of the real beautiful thing as set before by Garland Anderson but whose glorious crystal joyous beauty was Christ himself. Through and beyond his mellow negro voice and words was that tremendous great white thing that wanted to engulf you. You wanted fearfully to give yourself to it, more than you wanted anything else, and yet you hang back a little, sort of afraid to take the leap, to let right go of everything, accept absolutely. I do accept it. Then those dirty little doubts nag, and rather than face them one slacks — evades, gets little silly nothings [that] come in and occupy your mind. You clean your house, do a wash, make a grate. Weed, cook, finish a library book. All good unwicked things in themselves and having to be done. But absolute earwigs compared with the great true things.

In the morning G.A. was at Clem Davies's church and presented on Healing. It was splendid. The biggest thing that he said was that making disease a reality made it greater than God and broke the first commandment. Health is perfect. Health never leaves the body. When almost healed, the health comes instantly to us, there all the while. It never left. On hearing some tremendous news that lifted them right out of themselves, people sometimes recovered. In reference to Lazarus, he said, "Jesus loved him"; they told him he was sick but he did not go at once. Then they told him he was dead and blamed him for not coming sooner. "Jesus wept." Here he (G.A.) felt Christ's human side showed. Perhaps he had one minute of remorse he had not come sooner. Then instantly his Christ self came and he cried, unhesitatingly, "Lazarus come forth." G.A. feels the humanity of Jesus far greater than believing that he was all desire.[...]

In reference to disease, he quoted the telegram, how if you get a wire saying your mother was dead and it proved afterward to be a mistake, you would suffer just as much 'til you knew it was a mistake, as if it had been true. You can suffer with error, and unlike the Christian Scientists, he admitted suffering was very real, even if it was not a reality.

The afternoon lecture was well attended. The day was very hot. Everything that could open was opened. He began with the widow and the prophet and the cruet of oil. "What hast thou in the house?" was the crux of what he had to say. He placed the woman as us, the prophet as the God power within. When asked what she had in the house, she said, "Nothing." Then she thought of her drop of oil. She had to bring something. He told her to burn vessels, not a few. She was to have faith and to enlarge her consciousness — all love, according to his rules through the Christ consciousness of abundance within.

The lecture and classes are really too condensed. The one thought crowding on another. One should have a pause to digest each subject. Why must even our religion be crowded out of space? Everything is jammed up in the world now 'til we are all mussed and muddled, rushing here and there, our jobs and thoughts and manners and morals. Nothing has time to ripen and is stomach achy and confused.

L. has just rushed in and rushed out. We jarred each other. We really have nothing to say to each other except commonplaces. She snags up every statement I make and reconstructs it, showing me as mean, wrong minded, selfish. Then I get mad and resent and spit back. So it goes. Why were we familied together, I do wonder, being so antagonistic. I know I am horrid but somehow she coaxes all my worst horridness to the surface. At my suggestion she went to the healing service by G.A. Sunday morning. It was as if she was doing God and G.A. a favour. She did not decide to go until the last moment and I had started already when she phoned, so we went separately. It was far better, each would get more that way. She has not mentioned it since. I do not know how it appealed to her, my unorthodox church. [...]

[NO DATE]
Mr Shades's summer house in Highland District is a lovely spot. Pine and cedar woods, 175 acres of them in the middle of a lovely little lake. Everything is done up Indian. Much nicer if he had left things raw but his soul rolls round Indian designs, Indian colours, Indian robes. There's a falseness about a white man using those symbols to ornament himself. The Indian believed in them, they expressed him. The white is not expressing himself, he's faking.

There is a horrible old man there. He acted the fool. A know-it-all, he announced facts as if he was infallible. His mouth tore down at the corners in a bitter rush. He said his life had been hard. He longed to enlarge upon it but no one gave him the opportunity. The house was filled with mottoes and receipts for good behaviour. The kitchen and workshop were splendid and honest. You pumped water straight from the lake into the dishpan. But the living room was detestably overdone, ornamentation galore. The owner was a fine generous creature with a love of nature and a love of order and a passion for ornamentation.

I've been thinking about sermons. Seemed like it was best not to know your parsons too intimately, more specially if you liked and felt uplifted by their preaching. The men themselves always seemed so disappointing in their living, and I thought if a man does not practice what he preaches I have no use for his preaching — but — St. Paul says something like this: "List, after preaching to you, I myself should be a castaway."

Perhaps a parson preaches more from his ideals rather than out of his life, and the listeners may be able to grasp his idea even better than he can do himself, even if he is unable to live up to his preach. He has earned our gratitude and respect by giving us his inspiration to work upon. A man said the other day, "I like Clem Davies as a preacher, not as a man." People quote something he did years back. Well, perhaps he would not do that same thing today. Perhaps it may even not be the same man's work to preach and to live his preach. Perhaps he is only required to give the idea, not to develop it. Perhaps he cannot and is not required by God to do so.

AUGUST 26TH

My sisters' lives are so high and unselfish and worthy, doing things for people all the time. I wish families were planted like nursery gardens with every kind of flower in a row by its one kind. But families are sown broadcast. Every variety in one plot, higgledy-piggledy.

AUGUST 29TH

Today the grounds of the Mental Home were very fresh and gay with all manner of flowers. Half a dozen men were mowing the grass and clipping edges. They ran mowers most crratically. One was a great nigger who grinned slowly and worked slowly. A lean young man who leant very far forward on his mower handle and [did] mad absurd little runs and jumps at the grass, a melancholy individual who stood aside from his machine and saluted when I passed, and when I smiled in acknowledgement of his salute, turned his back and scowled. I was exasperated.

Mr. McLeod asked if I would like to take Harold into the grounds and ordered him brought down. He hopped forward the moment the key grated in the door and fell over me with outstretched hands, aimless bleached paws that folded over and under mine. His four front teeth are gone and his grin fairly fell out. He was so happy at the idea of the freedom of a walk round the grounds with only me for keeper. We did the flowerbed and greenhouse. He named all the flowers topsy-turvy: fuchsia were bleeding heart, hollyhocks were foxgloves, petunias were nasturtiums. We smelled the roses and heliotrope, then fed the big bear and pheasants and laughed over the funny pigeons. Harold thought they looked like old men with beards, and I thought they looked like old ladies with feather boas. And

there were fish in the pool, and spineless totem poles and little
model homes. Then we went to the workshops. There were
four large light rooms, bright and airy. As we approached, he
said, "Listen, that's Spruce, the Masset Indian." The place was
open. At a desk that was evidently his own sat Spruce playing
on a violin. It was not a good violin or a good tune, but it was
very touching. He has lost one eye, and that was the one
towards us. He did not notice us until Harold touched him and
spoke. Then he laid down the violin and shook my hand violently and beamed. On his desk were many half-finished
totems which he displayed with pride. Then there was his
flute, and he must show me the fine leather case he made for
it. He took it out, jointed it and putting it to his lips, played
"Home Sweet Home." I wanted to cry down in my heart, but
on the top I laughed and clapped my hands in applause, which
pleased Spruce. I could see Spruce back in his home in Masset,
Q.C.I., the sun and the salt air and the fresh way-offness of
unspoiltness and his Indian home and freedom among his own
people. We talked a little of Masset and other villages, and the
other occupant got up and was introduced. He was a white
squatter, also from Q.C. Harold loved introducing me to all his
friends. I shook hands. Most of them had silly faces. It was
their eyes that told. One man said, "Is this the lady you are
always talking about, Harold?" And then to me, "My, he thinks
you're fine. I'm glad to meet you," and we pump-handled
hands. In the tailor shop there were some six or eight patching
and mending. Two good-looking boys were at sewing machines
but their eyes told you the same thing as the others there. They
were in the house for the "criminally insane," looking so per-

fectly foolishly harmless. "So pleased to meet you, come again," they said, and I suppose any new face and particularly a woman's is a change for them, poor dears.

We went to the laundry then, meeting others on the way. Harold told me who they were and what they did, and we all grinned and shook hands. The man of most apparent importance was ironing towels electrically. Harold pointed to the linen and begged me to notice what beautiful ironing it was. Nobody seemed in a hurry. It was as if aeons of time was before them. The laundry was slack because it had been wet and the clothes were not dry. Opposite the laundry was the bad ward. A man was waving and gesticulating frantically behind a barred window like a beast in a cage and there were strange unearthly noises. We hurried round to the front again. It was about ten to four and time to prepare for early supper and for visitors to be off. But I left Harold happily standing by Mr. McLeod. He does not fear and hate him like he did.

A TABERNACLE IN THE WOOD
1935

SEPTEMBER, 1935

[...] Sketching in the big woods is wonderful. [...] There are themes everywhere, something sublime, something ridiculous, or joyous, or calm, or mysterious. Tender youthfulness laughing at gnarled oldness. Moss and ferns, and leaves and twigs, light and air, depth and

colour chattering, dancing a mad joy-dance, but only apparently *tied up in stillness and silence. You must be still in order to hear and* *see.* It is you that must be still to hear and see. It is you must go underground to smell those live and perfect smells. It is you must be still so they can come and make merry in your stillness.

Pout and Carabana bred today. This mating business is very marvellous. Two creatures agreeing together, fiercely determined to carry on life to perpetuate the species. It is a godlike, beautiful, sacred thing, and we have lowered it to the ground, coarsened it and made it shameful almost. Mrs. M. has the most irritating repertoire of dog and cat stories. Sentimental, mawkish, shoving the beast up with a human concept of life and mussing up all the blind, sweet animal instinct that is so refreshing in the beasts with a foolish half human. All evening she poured this [drivel] into my ear and rammed poor photos of animals into my eye which was already full of sleep. I longed to stamp and shout "shut up," and she so kind to me in so many ways. I vowed secretly never to tell a cat or dog story to anyone the rest of my life. I wonder if I have ever bored folks that way about my creatures. The animals are so far above silly sentiment, it robs them of their dignity. [...]

SEPTEMBER 13TH

[...] I must have bored people horribly with my tales of animals. I shall never tell any again. I will try to be like the Virgin Mary and keep things and ponder them in my heart. There is a load to be learned from the creatures.

A dreary procession of turkeys is mincing down the road. [...]

SEPTEMBER 19TH

[...] From life: There was a father and mother, son and daughter. The father had a government position and drank. The mother had servants and knew nothing of practical housekeeping. The girl fell deeply in love with a Roman Catholic. The father and mother were bitterly opposed. Pap said, "You never enter this house again if you marry Catholic." Beyond religion there was no objection to the young man. The mother gave in — sentimental. War came. The girl's lover and brother went. The lover was killed on the girl's birthday. The brother got leave and came home. The last night of his leave, he and his sister climbed a hill. He said to the girl, "This time I got through. Next time I shall not come back. Don't be an old maid, Sis. They need a man around. Marry." He mentioned a man who had long courted her. The son said to the father, "I shall not come back this time. You must stop drinking." The boy was killed. The father stopped drinking and the girl married the man she did not love. Parents and young couple lived together. Son and daughter were born to the young couple. Old man and son-in-law have not spoken for years, though living in the same house. Grandmother, daughter and daughter's daughter are closely knit. Between the three males is antipathy and hate. Do duty marriages pay? Was it right of the brother to decide the sister's fate? No one has the right to impose his desires on another before they die. *[...]*

SEPTEMBER 28TH

[Incorrectly dated September 29th in *Hundreds and Thousands*]
[...] It seems to be a mistake for more than one generation to live in one house; parents and their children OK, but no grandparents

or grandchildren. They belong to someone else. It takes more than nice people to make a nice family. One bell does not make a chime. One family [can] scrap and wrangle, insult each other and cuss each other's particularities and yet remain a loving devoted family. Another can always be insincerely polite and mawkish and not family at all, just a bunch of scraps.

OCTOBER 19TH

[…] How curious that one should care so. It seems as if it is harder to have one's thoughts slighted than objects. My sisters are the most unselfish people in the whole world over their worldly goods and the stupidest over encouragement or interest in — well, that sort of thing, nameless and vital. It is too silly to come to let it have power to hurt so. *[…]*

NOVEMBER 1ST

[…] Vana is in whelp. I wonder does she know what is coming to her? Does some instinct prepare her for motherhood, or does it break upon her with bewildering surprise through the senses when her puppies' cries come? When she tastes them and smells them as well as sees the helpless creatures, does she recognize them as part of herself to be looked to like a sore paw? Or has she some higher sense, urging her to nourish and protect to keep the game of life going on? She evidently has no fear of what is coming, no worry, perhaps a little bulky discomfort and weight but no mental anxiety at all. Her mate evinces no interest whatsoever in the coming event. His instinct to keep life going left weeks ago, his responsibility in the affair is over. There will be no link of affection between sire and dam through the pups. There is no "we" in animal life. It is "I."

NOVEMBER 4TH

I dreamed last night that I was lying on my back and my left hand was upon my pillow with the fingers open and palm up. Near me lay a man on his back. Presently he put the palm of his hand on the palm of mine, and he said to me, "Ask Jesus Christ about it." What was I to ask Jesus Christ? The words have come back and back all day to me. [...]

NOVEMBER 16TH

[...] Three of Clem Davies's churchgoers died in one week. Dr. Davies gave a memorial sermon lumping the three in one. It was a beautiful sermon. When Clem talks about death, one almost wants to die. You can feel it like a bursting from a chrysalis. [...] Seems to me our attitude towards God should be about the same as the animals' attitude to us. We are stewards of God to care for His creatures. They take God through us. They only know the material; dim-dim way back perhaps they sense the spirit. The wild ones must. They have no intermediary as [do] the creatures that know man. He is their all. They speak to man in wordless sounds. Pray to him, praise him, love him, thank him. We do not know God's language, either. To us it is wordless, but God knows our meanings even when we don't word them. [...]

How thoughts come and go. Suddenly in an impossible place, one that you want to keep [comes to you], but when the time comes to pin it down and think it out some more, it has scampered away. I had a beauty during the hymn, and the moment Clem started off, it skedaddled and rooted around the rubbish pile behind my brain; [try] as I will I can't find it. Thoughts are things, they say. Does that mean they are running around half-made somewhere out there just beyond our ken? Clem expounded on the Sermon on the Mount and was fine. If only I could remember it all afterwards. It is like good food you taste. It is sweet, you chew out the sweet, roll it round your mouth and swallow it to make room for the next mouthful. It feels good when it has gone down, too. You feel better for it and stronger, but you do not taste it any more like when it was in your mouth. It is still working, but in a different way. Perhaps the good sermons of Dr. Davies are like that. The words have gone down beyond the ears into your mind. They are not words any longer. They have finished mouth and taste and went on into the digestion. You can't keep the words any more than you could keep the food lying in your mouth, but all through the week they are working through the system, sustaining life and building up the body. Perhaps it does not matter so much remembering the words — when one thinks back into the woods, they are not remembering the particular trees, they are calling to remembrance the *spirit* of the woods. Oh, there's the thought I had this morning! "The spirit of God moved upon the face of the waters," and God created the breath of life with them. That was the thing that made the whole difference. When we create a picture we too must use our God-given power to breathe into it the breath of life. We can only do this by drawing it from God, letting God breathe through us into it. This is a wonderful thought. When the breath of life passes through a thing, it moves. Growth is always moving. A little thing becomes a big thing. We do not see it happen but it has happened.

Clem Davies says, "Holiness means wholeness." I take it that if a picture was a complete thought, if it was carried out with perfect unity, every part so articulated that it helped to carry out the whole idea — fitted into it our place in the idea or ideal, satisfying not only the idea but the soul also—then that picture would be [a] *Holy Thing*, a whole satisfying thing that would immediately inspire reverence in the beholder.

DECEMBER 11TH

Life, life, how difficult! The horrible doubts that come, that brood over you and eat into the very marrow, turning the whole world into an ache! It was not their matrimonial split-ups that undid our friendship. It was this other. I wonder if they know it. Letters between us are a farce. *This morning's mail brought an envelope full of theosophical literature. Once it interested me, now it sends me into a rage of revolt. I burnt the whole thing. I thought they had something, Lawren, Bess, Fred, something I wanted. I tried to see things in their light, to see my painting through theosophy. All the time, in the back of my soul, I was sore at their attitude to Christ, their jeering at some parts of the Bible. [...]*

Real success must be this—to feel down in your own soul that the thing you have striven for has been accomplished. To this must be added the appreciation of the thing done by those you love and whose appreciation you value as being understood and right. The folks who gush don't count, the superficial observer does not count, the toady does not count, the poor-sighted person does not count, the person solely material does not count, the one who finds fault from criticizing jealous motive does not count. Who does count? *The person who counts is the person who has nothing to gain, who lets himself go out to meet the thing you have been striving to create,* to whom the workmanship is secondary, the spirit first; *the nameless something that carries beyond, what your finger cannot point to,* that repeats and insists to your soul and uses no words, is found in all places.

DECEMBER 31ST

After approximately six months, an answer to my letter to Fred and Yvonne. The first reading I smothered liberally with mad sauce. They had ignored my effort [to] welcome Yvonne with my heart as an artist and as Fred's wife. For so long I had tried so hard to mind my own business and go on loving them all for themselves, irrespective of who they were hitched up with, because I do love them all. But the second reading I steadied down more. Fred has certainly had deep waters to plough through. He has [stuck] with it and faced things out and his newspaper job is exacting and exhausting. Lawren and Bess wrote me for Christmas, enclosing a snap of themselves; they were in full motion, arm in arm, racing across a park-like place, both laughing. They looked silly. They always stress how happy and free they are. I wonder if they ever think back—but it is none of my business whether they are expressing real mirth or hysteria. They are trying to pretend they are happy, irresponsible children. How long will they fool themselves? Or are they really pure-hearted beings on a slightly higher level than the rest?

Nineteen thirty-five has two hours more to run. Then 1936 and what? What will the poor old world get up to? If Bible prophecy and its fulfilment are right, momentous things may happen. Everyone looks at everyone else questioningly, but nobody voices it except the rabid British Israelites; the people who go to meetings only half believe, even the professed adherents. Lizzie believes in it and I do. We go to meetings and read literature but we don't discuss it. She and I do not discuss religion. She demands her own angle and no other will she tolerate. The intolerance of her attitude annoys me. I may be wrong-angled but I believe people can come to the same essential end by different routes. Perhaps I'm none too broad but what seems to matter most, according to my lights, is sincerity. I have investigated several paths. Lawren would think this insincerity—being led away—but from each different angle, Christian Science, Unity, Church of England, etc. I have definitely learned something. Dr. Clem's rendering of scripture delights me more than any I have known, I think. His direct simplicity of interpretation opens up new ideas all the time. The orthodox church set stories at Clem; sometimes they hurt him but he goes right on. I believe in his sincerity. I think he is doing a great work and I think all the time he is mellowing. God bless Clem. Nothing could be more humbly, earnestly sweet than his serving Communion.

BECKLEY STREET

1936

JANUARY 3RD

I was awful mad with B. so I wrote a real polite letter but sharp and cold with hot spots. Then I felt much better; addressed it, everything but stamp and lick. Read Miss B.'s to me over again, waited twelve hours, wrote another, burned the first and posted [the] second. I annoy folks very much by snapping my jaws down. If they only knew how it clears the black out of your heart to spit it out, they'd be glad to take it and clean you up and be squared up each to each again. If they take your "lip" nicely (where they know in their hearts they have done you dirty), it makes you feel awful kindly and nice to them, love them far more than if you'd never let out at them but littled it up to sour and stick. [...]

Gee! That old fool and lots of others make me sick over the poor dears lowering their status to sixth-rate individuals, robbing them of their natural nobility of their birthright as ANIMALS. They must invest creatures with silly sentimental twaddle, telling you a creature thought this and this—silly human humbug. I think in their mute unworded way they must despise us and our patronizing. There is a no man's land where beast and human meet. We have a lot of things in common: birth, death, desire to keep breath in us, to be warm, to eat, to sleep, to produce our kind and help [keep] the affair going on. They have a great sense of comfort, but [we have] more for aesthetic beauty. A dog doesn't care if his mate is pretty or hideous; he may have a code of beauty totally different to ours. The smell of another creature means much more than its looks. I think a creature thinks with smell. I think smell is its first sense. How unresponsive our noses must seem to them whose life is charged through the nose. They can pick smells out of the air with their noses like we can pick sounds out of the air with our radios. Smell is the basis of all their sex relations. Smell is the link that binds mother and offspring. Smell, smell, smell. Destroy a creature's sense of smell and you have cut him out from life, more than sight or hearing cuts off a human. A dog smells her pup; it is her own smell, a part of herself that has got separated but nevertheless must be cared for as herself. If you rub a stray pup against her so that it has acquired her smell, it becomes her pup. When a pup dies, the smell of her goes out of it; then she loses interest in it. It dies to her. It is the living smell that counts. We don't care about our relatives' smell. We don't even know the smell of ours, our babies smell of powder and

soap and other made-up sweetnesses. They don't smell of themselves or of us. Vana was little perturbed by maternity. Once her
large family were out of hand—weaned, rather—her figure
tightened back into slim lines, her spirits bobbed up, eyes bright-
ened. She slid back into her virgin days and puppy ways. But she
remembers that the pups are her offspring, plays joyously with
them, never touches their food 'til the pups have had their fill,
does not push past them to get my attention. What of the father,
Pout? A growl every time a pup comes near him, no recognition
of blood ties. Fatherhood is a poor little thing and motherhood is
great. I wish I had felt it in this life. The stupendous wholeness of
it, it must be an enormous lesson in mellowing.

MARCH 5TH
[...] My thinker is too tired to think. All it says is, "So all the
rest of your life will be like this—me and the beasts." Yet I
like it best, really. I have lived alone so long. I am so different
from my relations, I jar, they jar. And the tenants? Good Lord
deliver me, I have had my fill.

MARCH 19TH
Women are so much nicer when there are no men around. Maybe
men don't think so. Quite dear women change over into a sexy
brag as soon as a man comes into the room, when before that they
were gentle and real. Enter the man, up go the temperatures of
their being; voices pitch higher, eyes twinkle, they are all a-quiver
with blandishments to catch the attention of the male. It makes
one kind of sore and a little ashamed. So often the conversation is
led by little, indelicate, giggly hints into directions you did not
expect. It is not good being squeamish, but on the other hand

why want always to walk on the edge of things, to peer over, pull back, do it again and look and feel so consciously brave over it? One's darned old grand[mother] made us beastly prudes — reaction set in — but we have not caught the steadying rhythm; instead of not swinging far enough, we swing too far. Honesty with no simper or giggle can do or say plain straight things with absolutely no indecency. It is the self-conscious simper that dirties.

JUNE 1936

It is not good for man to be so much alone, unless they are really big with big stores of knowledge to draw from and a clear brain to think with. That's the whole problem. A clear brain that can take thoughts and work them out, can filter and clean our muddy confused thoughts, can read meaning into things, can draw meanings out of things and come to conclusions. One that [can] converse with life and above all one that can forget themselves. The tendency in being alone and not having anyone to exchange thoughts with is to be always on the fence between yourself and yourself. Not a fence that divides this and that, but an aimless fence that does not end. Either end is unfinished and keeps things neither this side nor that. What's the good of climbing the fence? Just a waste of sweat when you can walk round the end and be practically in the same place. Nothing kept out and nothing kept in.

JUNE 22ND

[...] Yesterday those silly single spikes on top of the young growth bobbed and bowed to each other like gawky, immature youths. Today they are trying to straighten and brag who can reach the sky first.

Thoughts are the only things we really own. Nobody can steal them or kill them or even know them unless we have a mind they should.

Therese is a strange woman. I admire her and she has no fear. She and her father moved near my camp. I was very surprised last night when she and her pup came into camp about 8:30. They had moved that day and she was tired. There was a cold wind. I made a campfire and we had toast and Vitone. She is going away to Calgary to be married and she has not seen her man for two years and then only meagrely for several other years. It is a risk. I wish she could have a spell of his society before she is tied body and soul to him. She is easygoing but she has been so utterly free for so long and she is not very young. He could not marry sooner; he had duties to his parents and now he is free. She figures if he did his duty by them, he will by her. But a man has only to give his outside self to parents, his thoughtfulness and caring capacity to parents and as much or little love as he feels. But to a wife, if he marries right, it is his whole self, his soul, body and manhood. Therese is mature, has knocked about, an only child and her father's companion since her mother's death. But fathers? Oh, they are not mothers. I can't enthuse on Pa's — too almighty. I have not met Therese's. It takes courage for a woman to travel alone some hundred miles to a man she has not seen in two years and sparingly for a long time before and say, "I've come." If she had seen him often and intimately since they both matured and knew they were going to take up just where they left off, it would be a far easier matter. Marrying takes a lot of love. She has a strong sense of humour. That will help. *[...]*

GOODBYE TO LIZZIE
1936

AUGUST 1ST

*Lizzie lies among the flowers facing death. I wonder how she feels
about it. I wonder how I should feel if it was me. I can't believe that
Lizzie is dying. She seems so usual. Any minute she might go or she
may linger on and on. Anything would be better than that slow eating of disease. That is horrible.*

Some people don't get a chance to live 'til someone else has
died. That was the way with Lizzie. Dede was so autocratic.
She completely dominated all flesh in our house — five all
right but crudely dominating. She scorched Lizzie, yet Lizzie
adored her, fussed her to death while she lived, mourned
deeply and sincerely when she died and then started to live.
Alice and I always gave Lizzie precedence in everything,
acknowledging her head of the family though all going our own
ways. We all had our own homes and it's a delightful peaceful
way for a family to live — apart but close.

AUGUST 4TH

*[...] All that was left of the old Carrs stood looking down into the
quiet grey coffin. All the fret and worry was ironed out of Lizzie's
face. Every bit of earthiness was washed out and Heaven flooded in.
I did not know she was so beautiful, so dignified and so sweet. It is
good to look on the faces of the dead. They look like crumpled old*

lace that has been beautifully laundered and renovated. We laid the
flowers from her own old garden in the coffin. I shook hands with
Una. She was good to Lizzie and Alice is great company for her.

AUGUST 8TH
[On a separate sheet of paper]
"A great artist is one who says as nearly what he means as his
powers of invention allow."

"If I cannot feel an undercurrent then I see only a series of
things that may be attractive and novel at first but soon grow
tiresome."

"It is harder to see than it is to express."

"All manifestations of art are but landmarks in the progress
of the human spirit towards a thing but as yet sensed and far
from being possessed."

SEPTEMBER 23RD
[...] This is one way my sister's death has affected me
queerly — nauseated me against a certain phase of religion. She
was a good, good woman, yet her religion always irritated me.
Why? Possibly because she rubbed it in so. She worked very
hard at her religion from the multitude [of] books about prayer.
How to pray, why to pray, when and where to pray, forms to
use, places to do it in. I think it must have given her great trouble. Praying is hard unless one is absolutely, has absolutely
become [a believer]. She spent hours at it in a torment of striving, I judge. Perhaps it brought her peace. Her end was lovely
peace. Perhaps that was the answer to all her prayers for healing and everything. Alice and I burned and burned and burned
tracts on every conceivable method of prayer and living and

dying and behaving. It was sickening, cloying, cheapening, irritating. She read slowly. She could not have read and digested them all. One *ought* to sympathize to honour her struggle instead of revolting, your mind reacting like a stomach reacts to overcramming and wants to vomit to relieve and empty itself, so it can start all over again after it has enjoyed an empty rest. I took home some of the books and looked into them to see if I could enter into their spirit. But I could not. A feeling of awful disgust came, not at the thing itself but at the volume. Suppose one went into a fine wholesale confectioners and were urged to gorge on every variety, that same feeling would be in your stomach as in my heart after those books and pamphlets and receipts. I know it's wicked but there it is. I surmise Alice feels more or less the same, but being more placid, it has not moiled her up so. She burns them and that's the finish. The very ashes inflame me. [. . .]

Somehow when night comes I always feel a little more right with the world if I've run up to the hen house and plucked little Cockydo off his perch and sat him on my heart for a few moments. He has the most delicious paternal little way of chortling softly with his head bent down on you, as if he was absolving you of all your sins of the day before he went to sleep. Bantams are very talkative and he has a specially lovely way, a little "sundown finish off." Quite different to his boastful proclamation of the arrival of morning. [. . .]

The foghorn sounds like a discontented cow. It connects up with thick damp outside. Inside the cottage, the three clocks — the eight-day hall clock, slow and hollow sounding, the trilling breathless alarm clock, metallic. The fire is out but the air is still nursing its glow. The neighbours on each side are in dark, wrapped up in stillness except for the ticking of their clocks and the beating of their hearts. The heart of a woman we knew stopped beating today. Her daughter and her husband will be lying in their beds. Everything in the house will be calling her name and their pillows will be wet.

NOVEMBER 25TH

It is the supreme thing one wants. They want it so badly that you ache. The spirit moving, isn't that it? Movement alone is not enough. "The spirit of God moved on the face of the waters." Spirit is undying life. Life is always progressing. The supreme in painting is to imitate that spiritual movement, the act of being. Perhaps if one understood music they could approach easier. Everything is in the act of becoming. Nothing has ever quite become. [...]

DECEMBER 19TH

Life is cram full of things, millions of things to think back on, to wonder about, to expect. It's great fun trying to word them. They don't interest anyone in particular except yourself. Why should they? I was figuring out which part of my work each teacher taught me. Seems like I got something special from each, just one thing in particular. (N.B. remember to write "My Teachers.")

I s'pose the thing to do with this painting learning is: Don't worry, paint steadily, day by day, just to the level you know. Next day you'll creep on a little higher, turning steps tremendously felt for and risen to. Nothing grows violently but with steady pushing imperceptibly. [...]

HOSPITAL

1937

JANUARY 21ST

[...] Cockydo, my little bantam rooster, is dead. Such a high-stepping affectionate little man. He had such a homely, loving little chuckle and he did love me. He did not throw me in with his hens in love and admiration but gave me a place all my own. He loved me to lift him off the perch at shut-up time and specially cosset him, and then he gave his explanatory little chortles. He loved to come under my window early and crow from toes to crown; every feather of him crowed.

My fine little Pout has gone too. Maybe temporarily, maybe for good. My cracked-up heart says this is wisdom, the time has come to lose, loose hold, but my indefatigable heart cries out I want their warmth and love. The corners of life will be so empty and bare and cold without them, corners too small for humans to squeeze into. I do not say that all the creatures we love here we meet again in Heaven, but I think maybe we shall meet love again, don't know what form or semblance it will take. Maybe we are like children running round, rolling snowballs with our little love ball attracting all sorts of strong love lying round; love of creatures and people and flowers. Our own love pulls it out of everything like a magnet. When some of us hoard our little bits and keep it too pure and safe, it can't grow.

FEBRUARY 24TH

[...] I know a man and a woman married; the man is the finer character. I know him best. The woman has always treated me nicely, but I do not think so much of her. I dream of them often. For unknown reasons, always in dreams the man appears. Poor sort of person and the woman superior and most friendly, why?

MARCH 14TH

A new widow came to see me, one who had loved her man. She had aged years in days. Her eyes had cried all the colour from them. There were big furrows across her forehead, dug by sorrow. She is not an old woman. How her husband's death has hurt, and yet she looked so beautiful, more lovely than ever. I saw her a clarified beauty, still and holy. I never loved her as much. Women do love their men and lean on them. It must be awful to go flat. The ridge pole of your tent down and you smothered below, and can't see out or breathe. I have looked a bit at married couples and wondered. Some really do mind. Life is broken in half. Others have ado to hide their relief. [...]

MARCH 28TH—EASTER SUNDAY

[...] I think Christian Science, New Thought, Truth Centres etc. make people impersonal, smug and unsympathetic. They make one shut up tight, draw into themselves, ossify. Yet it would be horrible to have a help that hung around you like a necklace. It would be nice, though, to feel they felt you were a live being. Nice if they offered to help in the tiny ways not included in the salary [or] list of duties ... I am restless and empty.

APRIL 17TH

[...] I am detestable. I go up to chat with Alice and come home depressed, flat. The slumicky, smashed-upness of everything gives me jim-jams and I'm so dreadfully ashamed of myself. I hate the back door that always sticks and is open all night and the broken steps and table outside it and the load of wood in front of the front door and the toilet seat brazenly squatting in front of the front door and the smelly dog-torn couches and the darkness of the trees shading windows and the smoky paint and torn wallpaper and the front back and side doors all in a row, the lurid beforeness of the whole place, and I despise myself for the deep detestation of having to go and make my home there when Alice's got so much to cope with. I *want* to live with her and I *want* to help, if only it did not have to be in that uncomfortable, ramshackle place. Hard to heat, hard to keep, and Alice stubbornly determined that it shall be, just as it is, forever and ever. No alteration, no improvement; to her blind eyes it's perfect. It's unreasonable for me to hate it so. I wonder why I do. I don't feel as if I could ever work there. I feel as if it means the end of my life — giving up everything. Perhaps now I've written it I will see how contemptible I am and be shamed. And anyhow, the time is not yet. As long as Alice can keep on alone, she will and will want to. Why do I sauce myself with dread ahead? Perhaps the operation will keep her sight as at present and blindness may not come.

APRIL 20TH

Alice went into hospital to have her eye operated on tomorrow. Una came down. That's a comfort.

     [...] I have been sent more ridiculous press notices. People are frequently comparing my work with Van Gogh. Poor Van Gogh! Well, I

suppose they have to say something. Some say I am great and some that I am not modern. I don't think these young journalists know what or where or how I am. I am glad that all seem to agree that I am pre-eminently Canadian. Some of the men artists resent me being a woman. Think it's *infra dig* for the men to have my work recognized —"a darn woman's." It's all quite fun. *I hope I do not get bloated and self-satisfied. [...]*

MAY 14TH

[...] Ruth has gone. I did not know how blue I'd be without her. She has meant an awful lot these past months and I'm afraid her last hearing of [me] was a bare bag-beast. I ought to have given her a last joyous send-off. The phone was awful and I could not hear. Oh, Lor'! Crazy fool. Those flowers have upset me. Just ready to do anything, probably to take it out in an attack of bad temper on someone. There is nothing nice in me. *Must hurry and get to another Indian village. It is marvellous how they help to keep one in place. There is something about the great calm of them.*

AUGUST 4TH

[...] They are burying Lola Dawn today. She died of spinal meningitis. The bright sprite of Beckley Street. When I went out on my porch, her baby hand waved across, always laughing and waving her hand. The two grandfathers and the two grandmothers have come, and lots of aunts and uncles. They have been about for two days.

His mother and father are dumpy, the father deaf. Her father is a dear. It's been a dreadful two days for them all. When they can't bear the congested house they come out on the porch and breathe, and all the men smoke. Her papa smokes a cigar and has a pipe, and the brothers and uncles smoke cigarettes. The porch is so small, the tiny garden strip in front must have been heaped with ashes of smokers. Neighbours have been in and out with bunches of flowers from their gardens. The young mother looks so white. They are all very tender with her. Her husband's arm is always going around her. When she can't bear the thinking about the dreadful ache of Lola Dawn, she goes upstairs and he follows. The curtainless window is open wide. I can see her head on his shoulder, crying. How does she feel about it? How does he feel? He is tubercular, he should not give tainted lives [to] the world to suffer to die. Does he think of that? Does she? It is good Lola Dawn died, perhaps. She just had that little two years' job teaching those young parents of hers. Perhaps that was Lola Dawn's job. They have a baby boy, not walking. What will be his fate?

Now they are back from the cemetery. Such a crowd of them. All very quiet — in and out, in and out — sitting on the verandah rail, scattering ashes on the garden. What a long day. At last the grandparents are going. Her father holds her close; he puts an envelope in her hand. She keeps his hand, crying. He holds her like a little girl. He has such a dear kind face. He puts her down, goes down one step and turns and kisses her hand and goes to his car. He pats the son-in-law. The father's mother, a plain dumpy lady, kisses her son. The little deaf father shuffles away unnoticed. He does not want to bother people to shout goodbyes at him. The uncles and aunts kiss and pat. They are all sorry. They go out the gate and get into the motors. Someone has left a car behind for the poor sore parents.

When the guests are all away, they go back into the house, down the hall, and he takes her in his arms. The little lady next door has kept the baby all day. She runs in and the two women cry together. Then she goes back; the baby is still in her house.

The couple put their things on and lock the house and come away in the motor to be alone and quiet and to face up to life without Lola Dawn.

NOVEMBER 28TH

[...] Perhaps if one had felt the pangs of motherhood in one's own body one could understand better. Until people have been fathers or mothers they can hardly understand the fullness of life. It was the life-long building up and tying down to another's will, not being free, that bothered me. Perhaps somewhere else we will have to go through maternity before we become complete. Yet the mother women often seem to turn into stupid cows running after their calves, instead of gently mildly leading and impressing their calves enough with their maternal wisdom that they are content to follow.

Dreams — how delicious and irresponsible; such wild leaps in the dark and always a safe landing, everything so unquestioningly right in spite of times and sizes and distances and people being out of scale or out of period now with another. *[...]*

THE SHADOW OF WAR
1938–39

SEPTEMBER 24TH [1939]

[...] Why do we think of God so much and mention Him so seldom, and then shamefacedly? Ruth is modern. She thinks God

is old-fashioned stuff. I don't know what she believes in, she is careful to hide all that from me, but I feel antagonism and bitterness toward spirituality or sentiment. She is a kind woman and generous, but I am always knocking up against something I don't understand that repels me. Why does she put up with me as a friend? I know a lot of women over old for marriage. They would love to be happy yet they feel gypped because they aren't. They think too much of themselves to marry anybody, but a god and gods are rare and difficult of cultivation.

NEW GROWTH
1940–41

OCTOBER 23RD [1940]
Lawren and Bess Harris came to Victoria from Mexico and paid me a three-and-half hour visit. [...] He spoke little. I felt that they were both taken aback to see me aged and feeble. For days on end I have had a steady headache and feel very, very tired and old. I did write Bess I'd had a stroke. She wrote back a long description of her magnificent petunias. Everyone on earth is self-absorbed these days.

DECEMBER 24TH
Lawren and Bess came in today. Lawren pulled out a lot of canvasses but his crits were not illuminating, although they were full of admiration and appreciation. His second marriage has seemed to me to weaken him. He refers to Bess's criticisms all the time, and I have never felt her crits much worth while. She uses theosophical

jargon. But he looks to wife No. 2 to word his criticisms. *He seemed to pick on some small, unimportant detail and never to discuss the subject from its basic angle. Trivialities. [...]* I could have discussed things better with him if it had not been for the presence of Bess. His discussions were with her rather than with me and were about incidentals like highlight and a twig or two which he thought superfluous. His visits have been slightly disappointing from a growth standpoint. Some years back perhaps I'd have felt more exhilarated by them. *[...] Perhaps the best thing I got out of this visit with the Harrises was a calm looking with impartial eyes at what Lawren pulled out of my racks, things I had almost forgotten that stirred my newer and older thoughts together in my mind and made me try to amalgamate them.* It is prejudice in my mind because I know Bess sham-acted to her friends in the old days. I have never trusted her since. I always doubt her sincerity.

DECEMBER 31ST

Paul pervades the house. Paul, Paul, Paul. Typical of the present-day youth, self-satisfied but not self-contained. Spilling with careless slop over others' lives, indifferent as to who is splashed, who is flooded out; what is easiest for him at the moment is all that matters to him. Typical of present-day youth. A. waiting on him hand and foot. With a splish of talk, he says, "I will make my bed. I will keep my room." And the bed goes unmade and the room unaired and smelly and messy. Disgusting cooking smells creep up to my flat. Fish, onions, things Alice hates herself but cooks for Paul. His every whim is her law. "Precious" is her name for him. Her starved sentimentality is glutting on him. There is no repelling of her caresses. She and I never kiss and mawk. I think it is since Lizzie's death we gave up kissing. I got so angry and hurt at the cold dead cheek she presented without warmth or care when she came in and out of Beckley Street that I believe it was my suggestion we should drop kissing. It takes more than a pair of smacks to make a kiss. I won't do it any more than I will keep up one-sided correspondence. In hospital when she thought I might die she began kissing me again, and I hated it. Sick kisses revolt me. I said "Don't," and perhaps it was cruel. As a child, how hot with love I was, and then I had three ghastly, smashed, mortal wounds I could not stand up against. I let love die, deliberately starved it out—that was bad I know and yet shamming love—giving Judas kisses—is worse. Judas did not hate Jesus, only he loved himself more and he was selfish. He used a kiss as the easiest way out.

The act of kissing is nothing if there is not impulsion from the heart behind it. The griffons' great love-filled eyes look upon me, and I seize the little shaggy heads and kiss them real kisses. I want to kiss the silent moving loveliness of flowers; in their immobility they are more reciprocating than a cold human whose unresponsiveness repels. Possibly the whole business of kissing from a human standpoint is self-conscious and self-consciousness upsets the whole works. [...]

FEBRUARY 21ST, 1941

[...] This beastly game of critic all the fools play these days makes me sick. They cannot do *anything* themselves [but] give advice about how a thing should be done. The longer I live, the more I see that what Whitman and others say is true. There is only one critic for every man to heed—himself, his own soul. The average critic criticizes to [feed] his own conceit. He is afraid you would think he did not know if he said nothing, so he says too much. He finds fault to feed his own conceit.

When I was young I loved the old (not old men, who I never did like). Old women I was very fond of. I did not flinch at dipping into their hollow cheeks during one of their smothering kisses, smelling their old dry skin, my face circled by long tremulous hands, their wavering voices, squeaky love and the dull eyes peering into yours. Now that I am in that place myself, the very ancient are too ancient to care; squeezings and kissings are like third lumps of sugar to a cup of tea fully sweet with two. I do not invite and rarely give kisses.

YOUNG TOWN AND LITTLE GIRL

It seemed important enough to me, and the most important building, my father's wholesale business down on Wharf Street. It was a deep warehouse with a deep smell. There was a black shield at the front with gold lettering that read: Wholesale Importers and Commission Merchants. Father's little office was near the front door; he had a wicker armchair and sat at a table desk covered with green baize. There was a cupboard of pigeon-holes at the back of the table, and beside was Father's safe, on top of which was a letter press, an iron thing with a cross handle with two iron knobs which Father screwed down after he had laid one of his neatly written letters in it and somehow or other the letter was duplicated. The window was shuttered halfway up so you could not look out into Wharf Street, which would have

been interesting because of the great drays with fine horses passing back and forth. On the other side of Wharf Street in front of
father's store was a railing fence to help people from falling over
into a great hollow place of bushes and wild land. Beyond that
was the harbour and wharf. On the left of the wharf was the
Customs House, square and brick. Mr. Gregory and his wife
lived under the steps of the Custom House, and Mr. Gregory had
a beautiful garden. Their rooms and the garden were below the
street level, and the back ran down to a wall of brick, and the
water slapped on the wall and I liked it. Sometimes we went to
see Mrs. Gregory. Their living rooms opened on each side of a
wide hallway which ran from the Gregorys' front door under the
main entrance to the Customs office to a runway right into the
sea. I thought the Gregorys owned the Customs House and that
they lived down there so that they could walk right into their
garden and take a boat out the front hall if they wished, but later
I learned they were the janitors.

On the other side of the wharf was a long, low, red-brick
building which was the Hudson's Bay trading store. It had small
windows and long counters round the walls. They sold everything and had jars and blankets and boots and lanterns. There
were always a lot of Indians squatting round the Hudson's Bay
store. Indians brought their canoes right up to plank landings
here and there along the waterfront. Just across the little harbour
was the Songhees Indian Reserve. There were a lot of great flat-
roofed community buildings with earth floors and long holes in
the roof for smoke to escape. Indians did not use chimneys, they
had bonfires on the floor. Travelling tribes used to camp on the
Reserve beach. There were always glowing beach fires and
canoes drawn up and tents on the sand or over canoes. I loved

anything to do with Indians. The Reserve was a glory place for adventure to my imagination, but even had it not been cut off by water it was forbidden absolutely to children. But one could look across at it from Father's store.

Father's right-hand man was called Ross. He was tall and deaf and stupid. He had a square jaw and when he did say anything it was strained through a long moustache. He was all pepper and salt: clothes, hair, everything. He had a high desk and stool and was always writing in big books bound in grey leather and very substantial; they looked like Bibles and I don't believe, even [if] they had not been Father's business books, they could have lied or permitted anything false [to be] entered there. Mr. Ross had two high stools he could sit on, but he preferred to stand on one leg with the loose one turned around the one that was fixed. There were two plain chairs for visitors; only people who had big business came to Father's store. Father sold only by the case or the barrel or the gross. The store was filled to the high ceiling with cases and bales lettered in straight black letters, and what was in them was all mystery, though I suppose the great leather books knew, and the letter press and the pigeonholes were full of letters about where they came from and where they were going. I think it would have taken a thousand me's stood one on top of the other before the top of me would have reached them. The store was so deep; it was a long narrow walk between the boxes from the front door near the office to the back door that led into what Father called the yard, which was not a yard but a great rough shed with a high dirty window that let in only grey light, even on bright days. The yard was piled with empties, packing cases and straw. It was a thick place with a smell as grey as the light, and in the dimness you never knew when you would meet green and yellow fireballs which were the eyes of Father's cats. Father had dozens of cats to keep mice and rats away. He was very fond of his cats. Every morning he took a big bottle of milk to the store for the old mother and kitten cats. There were always kittens peeping out of straw packaging in the yard. They were shy creatures and never came up to the office. It was so dark back in the store that rats might be expected night and day, and Father expected his cats [to work]. Neither he nor Ross sat long by the big round stove in the office toasting themselves. Nor did he expect the cats to.

Father was a man who turned his corners square. Nothing rounded or slurred. There was something I forgot in the store office. On a long shelf below Father's and Ross's desks there were shelves, and on them stood glass jars filled with Father's English candy samples. After Father had gout, Mother used to send him a little stone jar of hot soup at noon. We liked to go down with the soup because one of the jars would come down and we got one of the candies. Tiny hard candy that would sit under your tongue for the entire mile's walk home. The candy was always hard and pure and English.

One day, Alice and I went with Father's soup, and while he was showing Ross about shipping boxes, we stood on his desk and stole some square acid drops out of a bottle. We did it very quietly and stuck them in our pockets and started home in a hurry. There were no pavements in Victoria; the streets were dirt and the sidewalks wood, generally two planks carried over the biggest rocks and deepest holes by trestles. We hurried from the store, hoping Father would not reach for the acid drops bottle and notice how few were left in it. After we had passed the Customs House and were on the trestled walk, we came to a large pot hole. I do not know if it was my idea or hers, but the candies came out of our pockets and went one by one not into our mouths but down the pot hole. There was really only one street in Victoria, Government. The shops were one storey high. I can only remember our stores. You went up sour, dirty stairs to R.B. Thompson, the dentist's office. He had practised such a painful expression to seem sympathetic that [it] had become glued on his fat red face, and his nose had those lifted sides that mean bad smells. My pretty big sister took me to Dr. Thompson's to have a tooth drawn and I bit him, and because of his initials being R.B., I labelled him Royal Beast, which my sister said was wicked.

Carts and buggies bumped along Government Street; the business part was only two blocks long, The shops I can remember were a dry goods called Brown & White's, a stationer called Hillen, Mr Spencer's who had a dry goods and clothing, all sorts. Mr. Goodacre's butcher shop. Sanders' grocery, the post office, a tobacco shop called Campbell's Corners with two bulletins where men read the news. Besides this there were dozens of saloons. The doors had sort of slat pinafores just high enough to hide men's bodies and faces but not their shoes and shins. They didn't latch. Men pushed and they shot in and slapped noisily shut. I longed to see through these half doors but they shut too quickly and a smell of beer and sawdust came out that was horrid. It was strictly insisted that we always look the other way when passing a saloon. Perhaps that was the reason I wanted so hard to poke my head [in] and see what it was that these slat pinafores hid.

The naval base of Esquimalt was three miles out of Victoria. There were always men o' war in Esquimalt harbour and there were always sailors coming out of the saloons. A few lesser streets branched out of Government: Bastion Street, where the courthouse stood, and Fort Street, which had a few smaller shops, Clay's cake shop and Tippin's fruit, which had very shiny apples polished on Mr. Tippin's trouser leg, and Mrs. Laidlaw's hat shop and a lot more saloons — the Beehive, the Bellmont and the Hub etc. After one block, Fort Street turned residential. After she married, my sister had a house with a beautiful yellow plum tree, a black cherry tree [with] fruit that hung so high it only tantalized and could not be reached, and a verandah covered with a big vine. It was because my big sister married and went to live at the top of Fort Street and you had to go through town to visit her that I got my ambition and saw the other side of a saloon door. I went to see my sister and was to come home by myself, the first time I had ever come through town alone. I felt important but a little frightened.

Suddenly there was a tremendous shouting and dust and noise and barking of dogs. A great drove of cattle from the ranges in the upper country had landed at the wharf in front of Father's store and were being driven over to Goodacre's pastures and slaughter-houses at Cadboro Bay. The animals were wild from the range and mad with fear of having been shipped. Men on horseback bewildered them by shouting and cattle dogs kept at their heels. The steers tore every which way, racing on the plank sidewalks and slipping into open ditches. Their hooves thundered on the walks and in the street, dust clouds blinded everything. I was watching the dogs keeping the crazed cattle from entering people's gates and into the store doors. They were almost upon me when I was caught up in the arms of a huge nigger man. "I'll take care of you, li'l gal," he said, and swerving backwards through the swinging doors carrying me with him, he sat me down on the bar among all the shiny taps and bottles. And there I sat with my legs dangling and wondering which I wanted to see most — the bad inside of a saloon or the excitement of the frantic cattle.

When the cattle were past, I dashed home. "Where do you suppose I have been? With a nigger right inside a saloon. I sat among the bottles and saw the man polishing up the taps, but I hated the smell. I don't like saloons."

BRITISH COLUMBIA NIGHTINGALES

My sister Alice knew an awful lot. She was two years older than I. My sister Lizzie, two years older than Alice, thought she knew everything. My great big sister did know everything. Mother knew all about God, and Father knew all about earth. I knew more than baby Dick and yet I was always wondering.

There were a great many things to wonder about. Some of the wonderings started inside you, almost like a stomach ache. Others started in things which you saw or smelled or heard or felt or tasted. The wonder lived in them but rushed out and tapped and tapped until you let it inside your head, and when it got into your head it ran round and round until you asked a grown-up about it. Then the wonder stopped plaguing you.

Just before we were called in from the garden to go to bed, the flowers all looked nodding and heavy-loaded, the birds had called goodnight, and Bong, the China boy, had finished washing up [and] was starting for Chinatown, looking very nice in a cloth coat buttoned with tiny round buttons up one side and high up to the throat. The shirt was split up both sides and hung like the tail of a shirt which was not tucked in. He had loose dark trousers, a soft round black felt hat and a long pigtail of black hair, with silk plaiting in the end and bound with a tight little cord of red silk. But the best of Bong was his Chinese shoes. They had a soft shuffle and no heels. The soles were an inch thick and white and the tips were embroidered. Bong's face was pockmarked, his clothes lovely, and he was good right through and very punctual. And it was just when Bong came down the path and opened the gate, a strong high gate with a stiff iron catch and very tall poplar trees each side, that this wondrous noise began.

It was a strange sound and began in a little way, not like music but as little pieces of harsh noise, as if people were dragging sticks across little picket fences very quickly. More and more sticks rattled 'til it seemed as if millions and millions of people were dragging sticks over thousands of fences. "Listen, girls, what is that noise?" Alice said [she] did not hear anything special. Lizzie said, "It's only spring noises, you silly." First the noise seemed here, then there, then everywhere. Suddenly they would all stop, so suddenly it frightened you. Then all would rattle together again; such a tremendous racket that filled the world sometimes I thought they were quite close to me and sometimes the whole world was cram full of the racket except just where I stood.

I was glad to hear Edith call, "Bedtime, children." I wanted [to pull] the covers over my head. We trooped in to kiss Father and Mother goodnight. Mother was sewing and Father reading the paper. The big lamp had just been lighted and a fire was burning in the grate. As Father turned the paper over, he said, "Spring is here. The British Columbia nightingales are turning up."

"Where are they, Father?"

"In Beacon Hill Park."

Edith said, "Come!"

[The sound came] in our dormer window very loud. Edith puffed out the candle. The noise seemed stronger still in the dark.

I asked, "Can we have the window shut, please?"

"Certainly not, you stuff little girl. It's a mild spring night."

"I want to shut out the noise."

"Fiddlesticks. Go to sleep."

I moved close to Alice. "Alice, what are nightingales?"

"Some sort of beast, I think."

"They must be 'normous." Alice's "Umm" was sleep talk.

I tried to size nightingales in my mind by their noise. No matter how hard Dede pounded on our piano, it could not fill the night with noise like that. Nightingales must be bigger than pianos. Our cow was bigger than the piano, but even when her calf was taken away the moo-oo-s that made her sides go out and in were tiny compared [to] this noise. The ship's band in the Queen's birthday parade had died away when out of sight, even though it still played. The nightingales were beyond sight in the park but they were very loud. The cannon that banged at nine in Esquimalt so that people could set their watches right rattled the windows in Victoria but was over quick and was not so loud and tremendous [as] the noise of the British Columbia nightingales. To think the creatures were right were in Beacon Hill Park, lying in the swamp! Hidden by the bushes. Perhaps that was why we were never allowed to go there, and Lord it was boggy. I heard Father bolt the front door and then the grown-ups came upstairs.

"Mother!"

"Why aren't you asleep, child?"

"Mother, what are nightingales?"

"Birds—go to sleep."

"How big are they?"

"We do not have them in Victoria."

"But Father said."

"It is a joke out here to call the little [tree] frogs B.C. nightingales. Now go to sleep."

"Good night. Oh, I am glad Mother."

"Glad?"

"I thought British Columbia nightingales were enormous things that lived in the swampy part of Beacon Hill Park and I wasn't ever going there again. But it's only frog music."

MOTHER

I shall call this story "Mother" because it's all about Father. What Father did and said was the only thing that mattered to Mother. I wish I had known Mother before she was Mrs. Father. I cannot ever imagine her as Mrs. Mother because she died two years before Father, so we never knew her apart from him. And Auntie, who was not an aunt at all, came out from England a bride with her husband when Mother came out from England as a bride with Father. They came all the way round the Horn. This mock aunt said Mother was the sweetest little girl bride, eighteen years old. She had very dark hair and bright blue eyes and pink cheeks. She was small and Father was a tall, strong man. He had a beard when I knew him, but that was not 'til long after, for I was number eight of his nine children.

Father did not like babies. They were little and red and he ignored them as being beneath his notice, so we were Mother's babies only until we toddled around and looked with queer fright up into those grey eyes under straight dark brows and Mother primed us gently to say "Father." No Dada shortcuts. Then Father accepted us. Only once did Father accept one of his children in its cradle. It was Lizzie, number six. Edith and Clara, numbers one and two, were succeeded by three little boys, about a year apart, who each up and died after a few weeks or months. Mother's heart nearly broke. Those babes of hers meant so much, and she had to double parent them because Father did not help. And then another baby came, and Mother was so happy to have it snuggling in her arms, she did not mind that it was a girl. To Father, the new little girl was just "another," ever thoughtless of the squirming pink bundle because it was not a Richard or Henry or Thomas come to carry on the Carr tribe name. "She's like your family, Richard. That nose!" But Emily had grown so frail after her little boys died, to please her he bent and tweaked the child's nose. It got to be a habit; when he passed the cradle, he tweaked the baby girl's nose. But Lizzie grew up with an "un-Carrish nose," and when Mother said it was a pity, he was frigid and ignored the next three of us as we came along and left our noses alone. When, however, we were old enough to admire him, he took us one after the other as a pet, dropping the youngster above who [was by] then beginning to—well, to understand and fear the rigid sternness with which Father ruled his household. And [the] child ran back to Mother and gave her love, and Father reverence.

Father was a good bread and butter provider. Both were of the best. The baker baked him special loaves, four in one cottage loaf shaped two storeys high. It looked wonderful on the table and was bigger than the breadboard. The butter came from New Zealand in sixty-pound kegs and had the most delicious flavour. We had our own cows and Mother made butter, lovely butter worked in a churning big wooden bowl with a beautiful shell print on top of each pat. But that we used for cooking, because Father fancied the New Zealand butter. People came to our house and raved about the Carr's grand homemade bread and butter, and we children pinched each other and giggled.

In meat, Father did his family well too. The butcher knew Father and saved him all the best and most expensive cuts. Father said a joint under twenty pounds was not worth eating. His favourite was saddle of mutton, and we had one nearly every Saturday, roasted in front of an open fire in a tin oven on legs having a round pan to catch the drippings, and a clock thing that wound up and kept the joint turning and turning continually in front of the fire. There was a door in the tin oven, and Mother opened it and ladled the fat from the pan over the joint to baste it. The cooking of the saddle of mutton was quite a ritual. Mother or one of my big sisters had to attend to it personally. It was not left to the China boy, because Father would not tolerate Chinese cooking. And Father's stomach meant a great deal to him. What he had must be the best and it must be perfectly cooked. He sat at the head of the table — his end was distinctly "head" — and carved expertly the saddle of mutton and fat home-grown fowl, home-grown veal, home-cured pork. Father was fond of beefsteak too. It must be a perfect steak, perfectly cooked and perfectly served, that was lying on a great pewter hot-water dish. There was a little door in the rim through which you filled the dish with boiling water and placed the steak broiled over coals.

There was also a pewter hot-water plate for Father to eat off. These vessels had come round the Horn with Father. If they were not filled with water absolutely boiling, Mother heard about it. If the steak was not tender, the butcher, Mr. Goodacre, heard about it, and the family there on each side of the table looked into our plates not daring to speak ourselves and wishing Father wouldn't. Mother at the bottom of the table served the vegetables and pudding and pound tea and looked hurt when the stomaching God at the other end of the table raved. Only if things were exactly right did Father eat in silence. If they were superlatively right, he complimented his own growing or his butcher. Never his womenfolk.

There was a certain set of table mats made of straw or reeds, and when Father had been particularly naughty, it was my delight to put the whole mat family on the table when I was old enough to set table. These mats enraged him. He would seize and hurl them into the fireplace. We all looked into our plates hard and kicked each other under the table.

I don't know when Father's gout started, but as we grew bigger the gout got stronger and took a harder hold on Father's temper. And that wore Mother. And by and by she was too ill to get up at all. She had mothered Father's nine children and roasted his saddle of mutton and heated his pewter dishes and nursed his gout and dragged herself after him on Sunday rounds to visit every apple tree and primrose root and watched and warned us children, "It is nearly time for Father to be home. Are all the gates shut?" She wore out, and the doctor came every day and the bishop very often, and my oldest sister took on the hot dishes and saddle of mutton, and my next sister cleared out by marriage, and we four young ones began to see. Each had taken their turn at Father-hero-worship and had outgrown it. We revered Father; he was an honourable, very much respected citizen, but the glamour of almightiness wore off more or less according [to] the disposition of each growing child.

All the while Mother was slowly, slowly slipping away. Father grew more and more silent except when he was storming [at] one or the other of us. He missed Mother being about, although his daughters attended to his steaks and saddles of mutton. After he had tended his grapevine and his garden, he went upstairs and sat by Mother's bedside for a short while in a comfortable chair, saying little. He gave her everything that could be bought in the way of medical care, a good funeral, the best cemetery plot that could be bought. There he sat night after night, reading his paper, very stern and quiet. Sometimes he talked of his approaching three score years and ten. He had bad spells of gout, and a year after Mother died, he closed out his wholesale business. His desk and office clock were set up in the little room that had been our playroom, and he spent his time sitting at it and pottering in his garden. But he was never quite the same after Mother went. His death took place two years after hers. In his stern selfish way, he had allowed her to be the hub about which his life turned.

A DREAM

An old woman of sixty-eight, I dreamed that I was young and beautiful. I was dressed in blue, everything about me was lovely:

clothes, figure, youngness, and I was good. I had just come back from a journey and I had two trunks full of dainty clothes. I came into a cheap little wooden building which was a Roman Catholic chapel. I went into a little side room of this chapel, a room partitioned off from the chapel, but the partition did not rise to the ceiling. I took a little dish of communion bread to the young priest there. I carried the wine cup to him too. The young priest and I were both very reverent in our hearts over these things. Then I came out and passed through the chapel. The pews were full. I passed through and went up somewhere to my room where my trunks stood. I looked through the trays for a pair of gloves to wear, for I was going down to serve in the chapel. A girl came to me there. She said rather sadly, "Oh! You have served the priest. There were five of us who used to do it." And then somehow I was aware of a lovely voice in my throat. I wanted to sing. I thought I could sing in the service and I wondered about having my voice trained. All through the dream, I was very conscious of the delight of youth and beauty, of a lovely radiant personality and a beautiful voice in my throat, and I rejoiced in them.

I lay for a long time enjoying the aftertaste of my dream, neither awake nor asleep, neither here nor there. I returned to my old woman's body, tired, but resting easily in a comfortable bed.

LOVE

I fell in love with a thoroughness that was terrible. It was spring. In our kitchen was a small coffin-shaped stone. It was used for sharpening knives on, and sometimes, though forbidden by Edith, it could be used as a hammer. I had taken it up on the roof to tack up the grapevine and left it there.

"You'd better retrieve the stone before Edith misses it," said Alice. I ran up the ladder, the smell of Father's old grapevine young and sweet from spring, the exquisite joy of millions and millions of little mute white bells blowing on the cherry tree just below me. The birds' goodnight calls filled me with such joy, I paused on top of the ladder to sing a little, feeling closer to the vine and the blossoms and birds than I was to my own flesh. Then I picked up the stone and ran down the ladder. A young man stood there. I already liked him. When he took me in his arms and kissed me, my joy boiled over. Love rushed from nowhere and settled down hard and exacting. Soon I found the man was a flirt. I meant nothing to him more than a part of all the young loveliness of spring. Then I was deeply mortified and tried with dogged brutality to hound love out of my life, but its roots had struck deep, and it was to take fifteen years for the fierceness of that particular love to drive off all lesser loves. Silly, but love is unreasonable.

SOPHIE

One day, in answer to a gentle knock, I found a little Indian mother. There was a fat baby on her back, lashed to it by a gay plaid shawl. She had a full skirt of loud plaid material, a bright yellow silk handkerchief about her head. A little girl hung onto the mother's skirt and a heavy boy dawdled behind.

"Baskets?" She undid a very large bundle tied at the four corners and exhibited some beautiful baskets of her own make.

"Haho chuckiman"—(No money).

"Warm skirt just same."

"Haho warm skirt, next month maybe. Catch um Victoria." The basket I wanted was about 18" wide and 24" long, stoutly woven from cedar root and inlaid with designs in cherry bark and split cedar. It was square cornered with handles and a firm, beautifully fitted cover. I brought the woman into the studio to rest. We had a cup of tea and some bread and jam. Then the woman put the smaller baskets into her cloth, lashed the child tighter to her and got up to go.

"Take the basket. I will come to North Vancouver and get it when I get back from Victoria with my clothes."

"Just same bymby."

"How can I find you in the village?"

"Me Sophie Frank. Everybody know me."

This understanding trust, when I knew how often my race fooled her.

That was the start of a deep friendship. Something that touched the very core of life.

Sophie was the mother of 21 children, only six of whom I knew—she had already given birth and buried the others when I knew her—the three she brought with her on her first visit to my studio and three later infants. One was named for me. I saw Sophie part with these six, one by one. When life hit me hard, I went across the bay and sat a spell with Sophie. Her bare little house was clean. It faced the sea, and you could hear the lap or dash of waves on the beach at Sophie's door. Inside that door there was always calm, even after there were no more babies to roll round the floor as Sophie squatted there basket-making. I know that Sophie felt the same thing for me as I for her. She was a Catholic. I was glad the priest told her I was just like a Catholic and that she could love me. She was a little sad when she found that I did not belong to her church. So afterward we went to see her graves and the little Indian church, and I dipped my fingers into the little shell that held holy water and I crossed myself. I cannot feel if not according to my own faith that it was a mockery. It was gratifying to little Sophie.

When I left Vancouver, Sophie cried bitterly. She said, "I love you like my own sister. I love you more because she forgets me sometimes. You will not forget." I felt it a tremendous thing to be accepted by an Indian like this. I kissed her goodbye. "If you want, send word and I will come." She did, and I went.

After Sophie had buried twenty children, she broke and took to drink. Frank, her husband, had the habit for years. Coming from Victoria to see her, I found her drunk. The shock of having me see her sobered her. Her shame and crying were bitter.

Even the disgust of the vile-smelling liquor and Sophie dishevelled and wrecked couldn't shake my love for Sophie, and I love her still.

Although she has passed on now, it was just all comprehensive love. Perhaps to me it needs neither defence or explanation. The people in the village called me "Sophie's Emily." She herself called me "My Emily," and so I was. She is dead now, and the memory of her folded together with the little handful of things particularly mine.

Sophie had a friend called Susan who lived in the next house to hers. She too was a mother Indian. She wove a new papoose cradle every year and almost as regularly ordered a little coffin from the undertaker. I suppose the trouble was tubercular. Between the carrying out of a coffin and the weaving of a new basket, Sophie and Susan took their baskets, all tied up in cloths with knotted corners over their arms, and any remnants of their families still living came to Vancouver on the ferry, selling baskets door to door. They had a standing invitation to a cup of tea in the studio, and many a tea party we had. Nothing escaped their notice although their eyes never roved. They sat quite immobile, talked little, ate greatly. Susan was not so fine as Sophie, and according to Sophie's standards occasionally erred. Then she received a smart slap on the hand from Sophie. Sophie always wanted to be "nice." Often, if I asked why, she replied, "Nice ladies don't."

"Sophie, you passed my house yesterday. Why did you not come in for a cup of tea?"

"I came last week."

"That did not matter."

"Nice ladies don't come too often."

Sophie and I respected each other's "being nice." Our friendship was based on honesty and trust. We never pretended to each other. Many veils, of necessity, fell between us, veils of race and creed and civilization and language. Each stood [on] her side, sensing the woman on the other. We were the same age. Sophie was very jealous. If I went to see other women in the village, she got angry. "But Sophie," I said. "I like to know all the Indian women." She had refused to introduce me to Chief Joe Capilano's wife.

"You are my first," she said fiercely.

"You were my first Indian friend, Sophie. You will always always be the biggest."

The first day Susan came with Sophie, she said, "This woman got Injun flowers?" Indian flowers.

Uh-huh. She pointed to the wild ferns and little cedar trees in my window boxes.

PART TWO

Emily Carr gave three public lectures in her life, two of which were published in 1972 in a booklet entitled *Fresh Seeing*. The title came from one of them, the talk she gave in March 1930 to the Women's Canadian Club in Victoria. The second, titled "Something Plus in a Work of Art," was given in Victoria in October 1935. The third, the "Lecture on Totems," was also Carr's first public talk. She delivered it twice in Vancouver in 1913, on the occasion of her landmark exhibition, which she organized and mounted herself. It is often referred to in the literature and is published here for the first time.

"Lecture on Totems" is the earliest piece of writing we have by Emily Carr on the subject of her art and the indigenous peoples living in British Columbia. Art historian Gerta Moray, who takes a particular interest in what Carr called her "Indian paintings," has found that a good portion of the information presented in the talk on the meaning of the Native carvings and on Native culture was actually drawn from the writings of Charles Hill-Tout, an ethnographer who was president of the Vancouver Museum at the time. Moray also found that Carr used long quotes from the *Encyclopaedia Britannica* and a book called *Canadian Savage Folk*, written by John Maclean and published in 1896. These excerpts, which have been identified by Moray, are denoted by quotation marks.

The 1913 exhibition was a momentous event in Carr's career as an artist. Not only was it the culmination of several years of hard work and of her first major trip up the coast of British Columbia to the Skeena River and Haida Gwaii but it was a bid to present herself under her own aegis to the art-buying public. Her hope was that the main collection of Native subjects would be purchased by the province and that funds for further travel to complete her project of recording monumental carvings by the region's indigenous peoples (poles, house fronts and so on) would materialize. As Gerta Moray demonstrates in the manuscript for her forthcoming book, *Unsettling Encounters: The "Indian" Images of Emily Carr,* this was a bold move, and her failure was a catastrophe. It forced the decision (already being planned) to return to Victoria. There, Carr used her inheritance to construct a small apartment building, and she set out to make a living as a landlady while continuing to paint. The economics of Hill House did not pan out, however, and the return to Victoria became a retreat, not only from the art world but from painting. It was fourteen years before she took up painting again with vigour.

In 1927 came the breakthrough: the invitation to participate in an exhibition called *West Coast Art — Native and Modern,* being put together by ethnologist Marius Barbeau at the National Gallery of Canada. Carr travelled east on a rail pass, met the Group of Seven in Toronto and went on to Ottawa for the opening of the show. Before leaving Victoria, she sent Eric Brown, the director of the National Gallery, a short autobiography, no doubt at his request. It is dated November 1, 1927. This document, published here for the first time, is her first rendition of her life, and it contains most of the now familiar elements: her anathema for big cities, the negative response of friends and critics to modernism, especially hers ("they hated and ridiculed my newer work") and her dedication to it nonetheless. She notes that the paintings she did of Native villages were to please herself as much as history.

Late in 1932, Emily Carr, joined by a number of younger Victoria artists (Jack Shadbolt, Edythe Hembroff and Max Maynard), called a meeting at Hill House to discuss her idea for a public art gallery. She had emptied the lower floor of the building, put in a connecting door between apartments and installed an exhibition of paintings, including some of her own works, along with landscapes by Annie Bullen and watercolours by Lee Nan, both friends of hers. On December 14, about forty people came to hear her talk about the proposal for a permanent gallery to be called Beacon Hill Galleries. It would be a modest operation, intended for those who knew something about art as well as those who did not. And it would exhibit art of all kinds: "conservative, progressive, oriental, children's." It would be a "people's gallery in a people's park," she told the meeting, a place that "touched all classes, all nationalities, all colours." Moreover, she noted, it would benefit artists, especially "Oriental boys" (like Lee Nan, presumably) who were denied membership in Victoria's art clubs. The purpose of the meeting was to gather support and participation as well as to raise funds. A committee was set up, but by the end of January it was clear the project would be stillborn. In *Hundreds and Thousands,* she writes, on January 27, 1933: "The People's Gallery scheme is over for the present. It was a good idea and I am convinced put for some purpose into my mind. I went ahead as far as I could; then it came to a *cul de sac*: no money, no help, no nothing but to let her lie by and sleep and some day she may revive. I don't know now."

Klee Wyck was the first of Emily Carr's books, published in 1941 by Oxford University Press in Toronto and in print continuously for more than sixty years. Clarke, Irwin & Company reissued it in an educational edition in 1951 (and as a paperback in 1962), after removing an entire story, "Martha's Joey" (restored in 1993 in the version of *Klee Wyck* in *The Complete Writings of Emily Carr*), deleting the ending of "Friends," and cutting the ending with the details of Nuu-chah-nulth burial customs from "Ucluelet." Also removed from "Ucluelet" were many comments that reflect negatively on missionaries, such as the statement of one when it finally comes out that Mrs. Wynook's husband dislikes having his picture made for fear he will be trapped in the image:

"They have such silly notions,' said the Missionary."

A descriptive passage about the missionaries retiring to bed was also removed:

The Missionaries folded their clothes, paired their shoes, and put on stout nightgowns. Then, one on each side of the bed, they sank to their knees on the splintery floor and prayed some more, this time silent, private prayers. The buns now dangled in long plaits down their backs and each bowed head was silhouetted against a sputtering candle that sat on an upturned apple-box, one on either side of the bed, apple-boxes heaped with devotional books.

Just a paragraph later was another cut, part of the third sentence below about the missionaries changing their underwear on Sunday:

Every day might have been a Sunday in the Indian village. At Toxis only the seventh day was the Sabbath. Then the Missionaries changed their "undies" and put lace jabots across the fronts of their "ovies," took an hour longer in bed in the morning, doubled their doses of coffee and prayers, and conducted service in the school house. *[...]*

The cuts in these two stories were not restored in *The Complete Writings* but the major deletions and the whole of "Martha's Joey" are republished here. Ostensibly, these excisions were made in consideration of the young readers of the educational edition. However, the political tone of a piece like "Martha's Joey" is so obvious and the pathos of the story so profound that its deletion can only have been motivated by racism.

In the original "Tanoo" in *Klee Wyck* were several significant comments about missionaries, priests and the Catholic Church that subsequently were taken out. Carr was visiting the old village of T'anuu with her friends Louisa and Jimmie (Clara and William Russ in real life) and the daughter of the missionary. Standing beside a pole that belonged to her grandmother, Louisa recounts the story carved on it as if she had half forgotten it. Carr wrote in the original:

Perhaps she had forgotten some, but perhaps it was the missionary's daughter being there that made her want to forget the rest. The missionaries laughed at the poles and said they were heathenish.

In the next paragraph, in which Carr comments, "The feelings Jimmie and Louisa had in this village of their own people must have been quite different from ours," the latter half of the next sentence was deleted:

> They must have made my curiosity and the missionary girl's sneer seem small.

When night comes, Jimmy and Louisa go to sleep in their canoe offshore to escape the bugs while Carr and the young girl are left to sleep in a tent on the beach. Carr wanted to leave the tent flaps open,

> But Miss Missionary wanted them tied tight shut to keep everything out.

A little farther on, two entire paragraphs were chopped:

> The Indians would not do a thing for Miss Missionary. They let her collect rushes for her own bed and carry things. The Mission house in their home village stood on the hill and looked down on the Indians. But here all of us were on the dead level, all of us had the same mosquito-tormented skins and everything in common, and were wholly dependent on the Indians' knowledge and skill.
>
> I often wondered what Louisa and the white girl talked about while I was away from them working. Because of the mosquitoes, they tied their heads up in towels and were frightfully hot. I offered Miss Missionary some of the mosquito stuff a miner had told me of—bacon fat (it must be rancid) and turpentine. She refused—she said I looked so horrible dripping with it. She was bumped all over with bites. If you drew your hand down your face it was red with the blood the brutes had stolen from you.

Later on, when Jimmie and Louisa catch a devilfish for supper, there is an excision about the reactions of "Miss Missionary," who would not eat it:

> Miss Missionary ate bread and jam.
> "Father would not like me to eat devil," she said.
> She told me the hunt was a disgusting performance. The devilfish were in the puddles around the rocks at low tide. When they saw people come, they threw their tentacles around the rocks and stuck their heads into the rocky creases; the only way to make them let go was to beat their heads in when you got the chance.

And, finally, in the second-last section of "Tanoo," Carr's complaint about the missionary's daughter, in which Louisa collaborates, was deleted:

> When we boarded the boat the missionary girl put her clumsy foot through my light cedar drawing board. Nothing about her balanced—her silly little voice and her big foot; her pink and white face and big red hands. I was so mad about my board that I looked across the water for fear I'd hit her. Louisa's voice in my ear said,
> "Isn't she clumsy and isn't she stupid!"

In the first published version of "Sophie," when Sophie answers Emily's question about when the funeral will be for one of her children who died, she says:

> "I dunno. Pliest go Vancouver. He not come two more day. S'pose I got lots money he come quick. No hully up, except fo' money."

The last two sentences were dropped in subsequent editions, as was the description of the little Catholic church on the North Vancouver reserve:

> The smell of the church seemed fusty after the fresh sea air outside, the paper flowers artificial.
> The rope of the bell dangled dead in the entrance. It was a new rope and smelt of tar. Paper flowers stood stiffly before the Virgin.

The reason for this last deletion is not clear but would seem to have to do with preserving a positive image of Christianity generally. However, the expurgated passage at the end of "Friends" and the story "Martha's Joey" were obviously problematic for the white audience as they ran counter to prevailing prejudices and mentioned the unmentionable. Carr was stepping over a line when she declared that were she Louisa, she would refuse to send her sickly son to residential school. And Carr was probably breaking several taboos, social and political, when she pointed to the hypocritical attitudes of the authorities: while they considered it beneficial for Native people to associate with whites, they did not consider it good for their own children to mix with Native children. And it was a very long way beyond the pale for any Native woman to raise a white child as Martha was raising and loving Joey. These stories reveal a great deal about Carr's ideas on race and her attitudes toward indigenous culture. It is there in the language (in words like "primitive" and "nigger") and in passing comments such as Native people being "born campers." It is there in the situations and characters she describes. Naturally, these reflect back on Carr's own time and society, but the handling of these controversial passages reflects equally on the editors who came along afterward.

My object in making this collection of totem pole pictures has been to depict these wonderful relics of a passing people in their own original setting: the identical spots where they were carved and placed by the Indians in honour of their chiefs. These poles are fast becoming extinct. Each year sees some of their number fall, rotted with age; others bought and carried off to museums in various parts of the world; others, alas, burned down for firewood. In some instances the Indians are becoming ashamed of them, fearing that the white people whom they are anxious to resemble will regard them as paganish and will laugh at them, and they are threatening to burn them down

Now comes the question what *are* totems? Primitive peoples the world over have used the totem system, expressing them in a variety of different ways, carving them upon rocks, tattooing them upon their persons, making clay and earth images of them, painting them on houses, carving them on posts, but these high elaborately carved cedar columns, "totem sticks" as the Indians call them, are peculiar to the North West Coast of North America, to the adjacent islands and, following up the main rivers, they extend into Alaska and were formerly used near Vancouver. A Squamish Indian tells me that the old villages of Squamish had a great many lodge poles, but that many years ago there was a great log jam in the river which caused it to overflow its banks and all the houses and poles were swept away. One reason for these high poles following this particular region is, probably, that it is the home of the American white cedar [yellow cedar], which along this coast grows to an enormous size, not uncommonly having a diameter of from 15–20 feet near the base. I shall here quote from Hill-Tout on the uses of the tree to the Indians.

"This cedar has a unique and far reaching influence on the lives of these Coast tribes of Indians; it has been more potent in shaping their lines of culture than any other single factor of their environment: it was to them what the coconut palm was to the South Sea Islanders. From its outer bark men construct their ropes and lines, covering for dwellings, slow matches of 'travelling fire' and many other things. From its inner bark the women wove garments for themselves and their children, made beds and pillows, padded their babies' cradles, formed the compressing bands and pads to deform children's heads. From its *wood* the men built their family communal dwellings, made such primitive furniture as they needed—tubs, pots, kettles, bowls, dishes and platters; fashioned their buoyant and graceful fishing and war canoes, their coffins, treasure chests, ceremonial masks, heraldic emblems etc. The *branches* of the younger trees made their most lasting whithies and from its split roots the women constructed their beautiful watertight baskets. There was practically no part of this wonderful tree they did not use; even resorting to it for *food* in times of famine, robbing the squirrels and chipmunks of their stores of *cones* for the nourishment they possessed." And it was, then, from the *tallest, finest, straightest* specimens of this tree that they carved these wonderful totem poles.

By totemic marks, the various families of a tribe of Indians denote their affiliation. A guardian spirit has been selected by the progenitor of a family from some object in the zoological chain; the representative device is called a "totem." Indians were proud of their totems and were prone to surround them with attributes of *bravery, strength and talent,* powers of *endurance* or other qualities. A warrior's totem never lacked honour in the reminiscences and the mark was put upon his grave post. In his funeral pictograph, he invariably sinks his personal name in that of his totem or family name.

"The natives of this Dominion, then, in common with some of the tribes of the United States and other countries, have this system of kinship, which extends far beyond their own family and is known as totemism. The tribes are divided into *clans, bands or gontos* each having its own distinct crest or emblem of ancestry, which constitutes a native heraldry, or bond of brotherhood. The crests are in the form of animals, birds or fishes which are believed in a sense to *be their ancestors.* 'A totem is a class of material object which a savage regards with superstitious respect believing that there exists between him and every member of that clan an intimate and altogether special relation.' They make a theoretical claim of descent from the animals which they accept as their totems. And confounding the *ideal* with the *real,* they have come to speak of them as their ancestors. In a general sense those animals which inspired *fear, affection* or seemed to possess a high degree of intelligence or superhuman capabilities were regarded as their kindred, but those which lacked such qualities were despised or rejected as totems. The clan system with its totems developed a clan brotherhood with very strong ties. The duties of clanship consisted in making a common defence *against enemies, prohibition of marriage* within the clan, the establishment of a *common burial* place, the right of *electing and deposing* chiefs, the *bestowment of names* and the *adoption of strangers* into the clan; each clan was known by the name of its totem, as the wolf clan, eagle clan, bear clan etc. Different degrees of rank or dignity were attached to different totems. The bear, tortoise, and wolf were the three held in the highest esteem by the Iroquois. It is forbidden to *kill or eat the totem,* and this religious ban is known as tabooism. Although these people would not have hesitated in bygone years to commit great acts of cruelty, they would not dare to kill or eat their totem believing it to be one of their kindred or part of themselves. Only by mistake or in cases of extreme hunger would they eat it, lest they die. Some of the tribes believe that they are possessed by the animal whose totem they bear; among some of the tribes of British Columbia, not only will a man not kill his totem, but if he sees another slay it, he will demand compensation."

It was believed that the clan partook of the nature of the animal totems, the bears being very ill-tempered, the cranes having loud voices, the loons always wearing wam-pum round their throats to resemble the collar of the loon. The origin of *perpetuating the mythological clan names,* family history and *individual exploits* upon totemic columns is unknown, but it is believed that a spirit revealed to one of the chiefs, in the days when people lived in cold huts, the plan of a house in detail. The chief commanded material to be collected for the construction of such a house. And just before the work of erection commenced, the spirit again appeared to the chief with the same plan, but with the addition of a carved column placed in front; his crest (the raven) was carved on top. Underneath the raven was the eagle, his wife's crest, lower again the crest of his father and mother, and also the crests of his wife's family. The chief built his house accordingly, and thereafter all the tribes did the same.

"If a native exhibits his totem by putting it on his forehead or otherwise, all those belonging to the *same totem* must do honour to it and cast property before it." One of the same totem is due not only *hospitality*, but such treatment as would be accorded to a *close blood relation*. "As a primitive form of society, totemism, united members of a clan as brothers and sisters, extending far beyond the limits of family relationship, including people who spoke *different dialects* and forming a *clan of brotherhood* stronger than family life. Rival totems made war with each other, a husband and wife might belong to different totems which will divide them when a totem feud arises.

"*Mother right* prevails among the Western Tribes and in a general way among the Northern tribes of B.C. *Paternal right* exists generally among Southern peoples. By the law of descent the children belong to the clan of the mother, not that of the father. Among the Haida of B.C. the children belong to the totem clan of the mother, but if the clan of the father is reduced in numbers the child may be given to the sister of the father to rear. It is then spoken of as belonging to the paternal aunt and belongs thus to the clan of the father. Among Western Dene, titles and landed property cannot pass by hereditary into a different clan, and children of a noble belonging to the mother's clan could not inherit the property of the father. If the father had nephews by a sister, one of them became his successor. In order that the children of a noble might not be entirely disinherited, one of his daughters would be united in marriage to her inheriting maternal first cousin. The husband becomes a member of the clan of his wife a short time after marriage, by assuming the house and crest of his father-in-law. The crest descends upon his children, his daughters retaining it but his sons lose it as they follow their father's example by adopting the crest of the women they marry. The worship of animals was based upon totemism in its religious aspect. Many civilized nations of antiquity passed through the totem stage. Indeed, it seems to have been the first in all countries, traces of its existence being found in the Bible symbolism, as the lion is the animal symbol of Judah, the wolf for Benjamin, the serpent for Dan, etc."

The natives have a strong faith in the protective and guiding qualities of their totems. "This has made the B.C. tribes paint and carve them on their houses, the door sometimes being formed through the body of a totem: Charlevoix in speaking of Indians going to war says that 'they always carefully enclosed in a bag their tutelary genius or Manito, and these bags were distributed among the elders of each family. Before entering the country of an enemy, they would have a great feast and then go to sleep expecting helpful dreams. Scouts would be sent forth to note the presence of the enemies and these fierce warriors would peacefully sleep expecting that their totems would protect them.' The totem was also worn by some in the war bonnet to ensure safety to the wearer.

"The totem masks are the native insignia or symbols of rank and authority. Sometimes the pole refers to the adventures of the ancestor," as in No. 111 and 46 [references to paintings in the exhibit]. I saw this same story depicted on two different poles, each being carried out in entirely different designs. One stands in the village of Kispiox and one in Gitwangak, both up Skeena River district. The story runs like this: The Haidas of Q.C.I., who were a warlike and revengeful people, came up the rushing waters of the Skeena in their mighty war canoes and made war against the Tsimpseans. The battle was long and fierce and many many were slain. At the end of this terrible warfare, the Haidas returned home victorious, taking with them many many slaves and among them a chief's daughter, a beautiful young girl who was taken to Queen Charlotte's Islands and made slave wife to a great chief of the Haidas. She bore him in all three sons, the first two of which he beheaded. When her third son was born, the wretched slave wife determined he should not share the fate of his brothers. So waiting 'til her lord chief slept, she came stealthily and cut his head off. Taking the head, she placed it up in her canoe, and taking her babe she fled across the rough body of water—Queen Charlotte Sound—up the treacherous Skeena back to the home of her father. The Haidas saw her pass, but as the husband's head was visible in the canoe, they supposed him to be with her and did not give chase. One curious fact I noted: in both poles, the tongue protruded. Knowing there is usually a reason for all these little accentuated particulars, I asked what it was. Because, they answered, the babe would have died for lack of food, only the mother pulled the dead man's tongue out of his mouth. The child sucked it and so life was kept in its body. Occasional totem poles have existed elsewhere in Canada.

"In the village of the Ottawas the clans had different wards and totem poles bearing the crests of the clan were at the gates. But the Pacific Coast is the real home of the totem poles. Five hundred carved columns being known to exist in the land of the *Haida* alone in 1884. Alas, the age of the carved column has passed away; no new ones replace the old as they disappear. The ambition of the people now is to erect marble tombstones with an inscription giving name and date of death."

Old *legends* were depicted on some of the totem poles, legends that had always been connected with their particular family. These are very, *very hard* to learn. Many of the younger Indians do not know them; others again are unwilling to tell. Oftimes the old folk are blind and deaf, can't be bothered or can't speak English. It is indeed always an *honour* and a *privilege* to be taken in an Indian's confidence, for they are and have *good reason* for being suspicious of the whites.

They are also keenly sensitive to ridicule; very few, even for money, will permit themselves to be painted in a picture; besides which, for some obscure reason connected with "spirit," they are superstitious about it. They liked me to paint their poles, and were interested and friendly. In very few instances have I met with surly behaviour, though twice I have been met in a very threatening attitude and told to leave the village. They accused me of stealing their poles, but with a little tact and jollying on my part, and even at times a present of a duplicate sketch, we have always become the best of friends. It is my custom upon leaving a village to give an exhibition of all the pictures I have with me. I tack them up on the outside wall on one of the houses and invite them to come and see. I have known them even to leave a "potlatch" to come, and I find this little courtesy much appreciated. They love to look at them, right side and wrong, to feel and smell them, but always with the greatest of care. Never once has a sketch been soiled or spoiled. I often wish I could understand their Indian as they discuss them. They tell me they are good or *Hyas-closh.* One man remarked, "Well, I'm a clever man but she has me beat." I leave my coat, sketchbook and paraphernalia all round the village, much against the advice of the missionaries, but I have never once found my trust in these people misplaced, and I think they are keenly appreciative of the confidence shown, though I assure you I would not leave my paraphernalia five minutes unguarded in one of our villages with white children around. I have spent long days and sometimes nights in lonely villages with no other protection than the worn teeth of my 13-year-old dog. I never carry a revolver, being far more afraid of a gun than an Indian. There is usually a missionary in the village, but it is not uncommon to find the missionary has followed the people to the canneries, in the summer months, and the village pretty well deserted.

[Written on pages 15 and 16 verso of manuscript]
I love these people with their quiet dignity and I think they know it, for they are keen observers and sure readers of character. The first village I visited many years ago was that of Ucluelet on the West coast of V.I. It was at 7 o'clock on a cold misty morning in early spring. I was just a young girl and invited to visit at the Mission House for some sketching.

A very big man in a very little canoe took me from the steamer to the house, a lonesome little dwelling with its face to the sea and its back to the dense forest abounding in panthers. Indeed, they used to steal all the meat, ripping the wire off the safe with their powerful paws. Hipi, an old Indian, arrived immediately with five or six others to inspect the new guest. Visitors were scarce. He sat upon a table scrutinizing me intently but speaking no word. By and by, with his eyes still upon me, he began in Chinook. I think he gave me a better character than I deserved, but one point struck terror to my heart as the missionary translated, "Her heart is good and she is not stuck up and would eat clams in an Indian hut if invited." Alas,

I was put to the test later and was miserably found wanting. It wasn't even clams but a disgusting concoction, all sitting round the pot and dipping in their spoons. These people named me Klee Wyck (the Laughing One), for they said, "She cannot talk our language but she laughs much and that is just the same we understand." A name is not just a label to an Indian, but it is something real. Besides the common names given to them by the priest or missionary at baptism, everyone has his own special Indian name. I asked one man how they got these.

Several different species of totem may be found in British Columbia. "Heraldic columns are erected by B.C. tribes to commemorate the event of a chief taking his position in the tribe by building a house. These poles vary in length from 40–60 ft. and are hollowed in back and carved in front. The general name for these among the Haidas is *keeang*, but each column has an individual distinguishing name; when a chief decides to erect a keeang and build a lodge, he invites all the tribes in the vicinity to be present. Upon arrival, they are received by dancers in costume and hospitably entertained. At the appointed time the Indians move the pole upon rollers to a hole previously dug 7–10 ft. deep (the pole has of course been already carved and ornamented). Long ropes are fastened to it, which are grasped by gangs of men, women and children who stand at a considerable distance, waiting to haul. The strongest men in the company raise the pole with their hands until it reaches their heads, when stout poles tied together in the form of shears are placed under it as supports. Sharp pointed poles are used to raise it to an angle of 45 degrees and then the signal is given for the persons at the ropes to haul. With a loud shout, the butt is dropped; the column being set plumb is then packed around the base with earth. The crowd repairs to the house of the owner, who gives a potlatch, a big feast being prepared, and a great distribution of all his property consisting of blankets, trinkets, money. These gifts are distributed to all gentes except the one to whom the column belongs. The Tlinkleets, Haidas and Tsimpseans erect mortuary columns upon the death of a chief. These are solid circular poles carved only on base and summit. When they are erected, a feast is given to the multitude and blankets are distributed to the makers of the pole."

This collection contains many specimens of these mortuary columns. In Q.C.I., there are many poles in which the actual coffin is buried. These are thick cedar trunks and are placed in the earth large end up. In the top is a large cavity hollowed, and the coffin is placed within, and slabs nailed across the front with the crest carved upon them. Nos. [?] and [?] are examples of these burial posts.

"Several clans are sometimes united with a common totem. These are known as Phratry. The phratry with its common totem and interests embraces several clans, each with its own subcrest, There are several phratries among the tribes of B.C. This totem is a material object revered by a body of men and women who believe themselves to be of one blood, descended from same ancestor and bound to protect each other, on account of this kinship and faith in same totem. By means of clan totems the clan name was perpetuated among the Indian tribes as shown by totem posts where name of clan usually surmounts the column, family history and genealogical record being contained in carvings below. *Personal or inherited columns* are common among the native tribes of B.C. Early in life the Indian seeks a lonely spot in Forest, Mountain or Prairie. Here he fasts and prays until (in a dream) is revealed to him his personal totem, in the form of some animal whom he kills, preserving the skin so that he may ever have it with him to protect and guide him. He must never afterward kill or eat any of its kind. Whenever he goes as a hunter or a warrior it must accompany him to assure success and safety. If he becomes a medicine man it will reveal to him some herb as medicine that the other shamen know nothing of and he depends on its instruction to give him influence in his tribe."

Indians believed in a multiplicity of spirits — that all nature, in all her forms, was thus animated: every object had its own soul or spirit, which was distinct from the body or material form and could separate itself from it and live an independent or ghostly existence. Not only were these objects which we call animate — that is living, sentient bodies possessed of souls, or spirits — but also every insensate object. The smallest and most insignificant in common with the largest and most impressive, a blade of grass, stick or stone, the very tools or utensils made and employed by themselves, each and all possessed spirit forms more real than their corporeal ones because more permanent and indestructible. The material form of an object could be destroyed, the tool broken, the fish or deer killed and eaten, but the spirit forms of the object would still remain. Thus, the spirit world was very real to them, ever present, ever encompassing them, indeed the source of all the ill or pleasure of their existence. They were ever at the mercy of the ghosts of things whose pity must be implored, anger propitiated or goodness recompensed.

"Among the Salish of the interior every man and woman customarily had his or her personal friendly spirit or spirits, the methods of acquiring these seem the same everywhere. The seeker goes apart by himself and undergoes a more or less lengthy course of training and self-discipline. The course continues for a period of four days to four years. (Among these people four is the mystic number and everything goes by it.) Those taking the longer course are generally seeking shamanistic or other special mystery powers; prolonged fasts, frequent bathings and exhausting bodily exercises are the means adopted for inducing the desired state — the mystic dreams and visions. With the body in this enervated condition, the mind becomes abnormally active and expectant, dreams, visions and hallucinations naturally follow. It is not difficult to realize how *real* to him must seem the vision of the looked for spirit and how firm his belief in its *actual* manifestation; the spirit of almost every object might become a totem, a few only lacked mystery power. Each class or order of people had its favourite and characteristic objects, this applied particularly to the shaman or medicine men who each possessed many familiars and were equipped by their incantations to have great influence with the spirits. Their chief familiars were objects that had reference to death, dead bodies or parts of them, nocturnal animals, darkness, gravestones and suchlike. Warriors, guardian spirits, were mostly carnivorous animals, blood, thunder and all kinds of weapons. Fishermen sought spirits of canoes, water, fishing utensils, waterfowl etc. The women's favourite guardian spirits were objects used by themselves such as baskets, kettles, buckets, packing lines etc. Once a person believed himself under the protection of one of these spirits his first act was to secure this thing and carry it on his person, or, if this were not possible, to hide it in some place accessible in time of need or trouble.

"Dr. Peet says that human figures were used to represent totems although they were sometimes employed to show the mythologies which prevailed and when such [was] the case, a higher type of totemism has been introduced. It has been claimed that the monkey may be seen on the totem posts of the Haidas but no animal of that description has been found upon the North West Coast. The figure supposed to be that of the monkey being the bear with a human face and form."

One of these old mythological legends told me in Kispiox ran thus: it is in connection with pole No. 82. This pole represents a woman's figure on the base with a frog coming out of each eye and another out of the mouth. This is the story: A beautiful young woman went down to the water to clean her fish. She looked about her for a large flat stone to sit upon while she worked. A monster in [the] form of a frog had long loved her, but she would have nothing to do with him. She used to climb on a tree leaning over the water and taunt him when he would vainly try to clasp her reflection. So when he saw her come to clean her fish, he flattened himself out among the stones, and she, taking him to be a large flat stone, sat upon his back and began to clean her fish. Stealthily, he slid into the water, bearing her with him, and down he dived to the bottom where the fish were his slaves, the frogs his servants. The ducks and geese on the top of the water were the sentinels guarding his realm. For long she lived under there and wept and mourned to get back to her home and husband, but in vain. At last it was revealed to her by her guardian spirit that there was a certain weed which all these people were very fond of and which if eaten by them would produce a sound sleep (we will suppose it was a seaweed); she procured large quantities of this weed which they all devoured greedily and were soon fast asleep. She passed by the monster and his people and rose to the top of the waters, but the ducks and geese refused to touch her weed. Now up to this time ducks and geese had been blind. They possessed eyes, but the slits had not been made so they could not see through the lids. She asked these poor blind creatures if they would not like to see. Of course they said yes, so she offered to slit all their eyes if they would let her pass. This she did, but she was in such a hurry lest the people below should awake and miss her that she had little time for care and she cut them all crooked. That is the reason that to this day you will frequently see wild ducks and geese with one eye larger than the other or with crooked lids. But the woman escaped and got back to her husband. The poor fowls were too bewildered with their first sight of the world to think anything about her.

The Haidas or people of Queen Charlotte Islands are a particularly fine race of people. They are very clever workers and excel in carving; as well as the large cedar columns, they make smaller totem poles of carved slate [argillite] which they get from parts of the southern island. These are beautiful and take a very fine polish when finished. They also carve pipes, boxes and other things out of this slate. Of late years, however, there are very few people left who do this work and it is of a poorer type to cater to the tourist trade, neither so fine nor so true as the older carvings. These people also do beautiful metalwork, gold and silver bracelets etc., besides their fine basketry. The basketry of the Indians is a very fine art. Every tribe of people have their own style of baskets and various materials are used, viz. cedar roots, cedarbark, rushes, grass, birchbark, also the quills of birds and the porcupine. Regarding the purpose of ornamentation and design on these baskets, "to imagine them only ornamentation would be to misrepresent their true character and the original intention of the basket maker. The primary purpose of all design and representations among primitive people was not decorative in the sense in which we use the word but symbolical of certain ideas or to represent their totems and tutelary spirits, for it was customary to carve these upon many of their personal belongings and utensils." These ideas and forms are sometimes so conventionalized as to be unreadable to us, but the symbolism is clear enough to the Indian.

There is a great dignity about the Haida people. They take life more seriously than most tribes. It was interesting to note that the faces of their totems were more austere and grim in appearance. I only saw one smile, No. [?]. Up the Skeena River, on the contrary, the Tsimpseans seem to regard life in a more cheerful light, and there were many more cheerful countenances depicted. Another peculiarity about the two districts that I noted was this — the unpainted poles on the islands become very grey and pale pearly tints from exposure to the elements and their crevices become covered with moss, whereas those up the Skeena become warm brown in colour and almost appear like new wood, though on close observation you can see they are of great age and much worn. The Haida people have diminished vastly in numbers. I was told that whereas thirty years ago there were 30,000 natives in the Skidegate Inlet, they now number three hundred souls. A terrible scourge of smallpox in the islands wiped out many of their villages. The people have now formed themselves into two bands, the Masset people on the North Island, the Skidegate on the south.

The other villages stand forsaken. I visited some of those old places, and their solemn forsaken loneliness and dignity is indeed wonderful. Very few houses are left standing though you always find traces of the solid beams and posts of the old potlatch houses still standing. There was a terrible ceremony attached to the building of these great houses, for it was customary to put live slaves in the postholes and plant the post on top of them.

I got a Haida man and his wife to take me to Cha-atl. Up the Skidegate Inlet we went in a wide deep fishing boat with a gasoline engine in it. These people are ideal travelling companions and born campers. The trip was only planned late the evening before and we started at nine the next morning, but nothing was forgotten; even the cat came along, and the ease and method with which they made camp were astonishing.

The day of our start was perfect. We stopped at an old village and made lunch and I sketched all the poles left standing, some five or six in number. I never yet saw an Indian village that was not beautifully situated, the very pick of the land all about, and no one loves and absorbs that beauty more than the Indian. It has been my privilege to know some Indians intimately (and it is necessary to know these people well before they will speak freely before you). On asking them of the country (as to its situation and pictorial advantages for my work), I have heard some of the most beautiful and expressive descriptions of places, often times in broken English with Chinook intermingled. But it is more than the superficial appearance of the place they give to you. They have absorbed its beauty, its calm and its intensity, and they make you "feel" it. They are full of poetry, these people.

Skidegate Inlet is lovely. In places it is quite narrow and also very shallow, needing a very careful steersman; here the man stood upon the boat's prow and looked down through the clear water for the channel. No word was spoken; he signalled with his arms, the woman steered accordingly. There was no fuss or worry. I did not know 'til afterwards that these shallows were a difficult and dangerous piece of water to navigate. We were followed up almost the entire inlet by large shoals of porpoises who gambolled round the boat with mad antics and made a splendid sight leaping as they did right out of the water. Six and eight abreast on both sides of the boat as if at a given signal. They did not leave us until we came to shallow water.

We reached Cha-atl late in the afternoon. It is situated almost at the mouth of the Skidegate Inlet on the West Coast in a beautiful little bay. Many poles are still standing and many many more are lying among the intensely thick underbrush, moss grown and rotting. There are, though, fine specimens left. No. [?] is a sample of three large ones standing in the centre of the group. We were in full sound of the roar of the West Coast surf, that West coast of Q.C.I. with its fearful reputation; few venture round there. The sea is always rough, treacherous and wicked. Men who have seen it tell me that they have never anywhere seen such an absolutely wild, ferociously rugged coast.

The boat was anchored out a way, and we landed one at a time in the small dugout canoe. I made a quick summary of the work to be done and was already deep in a sketch by time the others were landed. Here I may say that this is one of the trying features of this work. Places are so difficult to get at, accommodation always meagre, boats very erratic. You must therefore come quickly to your conclusions, select your objects and your view of objects. Time is so precious you dare not stop to rest up or think how tired you are. In places where there is much walking, you must shoulder a very heavy pack. The elements always have to be buffeted. Wind, showers, hot sun, incoming tides. Indians satisfied as to why you've come, etc. You must be absolutely honest and true in the depicting of a totem, for meaning is attached to every line; you must be most particular about detail and proportion. *I never use the camera nor work from photos;* every pole in my collection has been studied from its actual reality in its own original setting and I have, as you might term it, been personally acquainted with every pole shown here.

Indians, I think, express it well when they say to one another, "Come and see the woman make pictures with her head and hands, not with a box." Many of them have spoken to me of this, saying it was new for them to see pictures made thus, though they have seen cameras and some indeed used them. For instance, when I was doing the poles in Hazelton, an Indian stepped up and photographed me.

But to return to Cha-atl; in these northern places, it is light enough to work 'til nine and after. After supper came the stories round the campfire; these people spoke good English. I had brought a young Canadian girl with me from Skidegate and we sat there listening to ghost stories. They seemed very real with the coffins perched up on the top of the mortuary columns above our heads, the silent black forest behind us and the melancholy roar of the West Coast surf in our ears, especially so as "Mother saw this one" and "Grandmother that." Then having well filled our heads with these tales, the pair got up and paddled off to the boat in midstream to sleep, for they said they would not sleep on the beach among the ghosts of the dead. We were left in our little tent alone in the silent blackness. We were certainly not troubled by the ghosts. Our bed of cut rushes was fairly comfortable, but we were devoured by flies and mosquitoes and got little sleep. Just at dawn I got up and walked on the beach. It was wonderful. The great stillness, the solemn old grey poles towering above the tent, the shorter mortuary columns crowned with their crested coffins, the water softly lapping the pebbly beach. And the sullen roar of the distant surf. These things redolent of the past of a strong, fine, primitive people are worth seeing and feeling. The trip to Cha-atl is full of wonderful memories to me.

Another most delightful trip was my visit to Yan (No. 77). I went there twice, spending long days among the poles. Yan stands nearly opposite to Masset on the northern island of the Charlotte group, with a wide stretch of Masset Inlet between. This body of water can be extremely rough and unpleasant at times, full of treacherous currents and eddies. I went in a small dugout Indian boat, and my companions were an Indian woman and her two children. She sat in the stern with the baby in her lap and steered as a small girl of 12 deftly manipulated the sail, a homemade affair of flour sacks. How well they do handle their boats; it seems born in them. It was a wild day and rained heavily and I could only sketch between showers. We sheltered in a hut and made a fire, and the woman told me stories of her life. These are always worth hearing, but you must not ask too many questions or the storyteller will become mute. Listen then: this woman had had 9 children and lost them all. Indian women love their children passionately. To have no children is to be truly desolate. When the last of this woman's died, she was heart-broken. Then came to her a young woman of Skidegate, her friend and the mother of five or six children. She brought with her two, a boy and a girl, and these she gave to the forlorn mother to somewhat console her. (It was not, the woman said, that she did not love her children dearly that she could give them away, for she wept many many days and could not eat, but she was so sorry for her friend.) What a sacrifice for friendship's sake. How many white mothers, though they might grieve for another's sorrow, would be even dream of such a sacrifice?

There is a fine type of honour, too, among these people. We sheltered in an old hut which was used at times by some Indians to store tools in (for it is not uncommon for the people to go back and forth to these old villages and use any cultivated spots to grow vegetables and berries in). There were a few old clothes, some tools and some dry firewood there; when we had finished, the woman, after carefully extinguishing the fire, sought fresh wood and replaced what we had used. Though they have much in common, yet they have great respect for one another's property. Fruit would rot on the branches in a garden if its owner were away, but the others would not think it right to pluck it for their own use without permission. I think they could teach us many many things, especially the old ones; the vices of the younger ones, alas, have been mainly acquired from the whites, poor souls! They looked up to the whites as a superior race whom they should try to copy; alas, they could not discriminate between the good and bad. There was so much bad, and they copied it. In their own primitive state they were a moral people with a high ideal of right. Here's a little story I heard at Hazelton. An Englishman going prospecting with some Indians was much concerned at leaving his belongings in his tent as he could not lock it up. Oh, said his Indian guide, it is quite safe to do so, there are no white men this side of Dawson. There were Indians all about but it never occurred to him they would steal.

There is a mighty calm about Yan. The great solemn unpainted poles with a carpet of fireweed running a wild riot of colour around their bases. There also are some very fine tombs, of which No. [?] is an example; a gorgeous red-leafed shrub which abounds here had formed a sturdy bush on the top of one of the posts. It is a very dignified tomb and one can well imagine a primitive noble buried within.

Among the tribes there are many different modes of burial, though it is becoming now more common to bury in the earth as we do. Yet many strange methods of disposing of the dead may still be seen. I have spoken of the method of placing the coffins in the top of carved columns. Much of this was done in Q.C.I., and it is only chiefs, shamen and nobles who are accorded these grand tombs. Just beyond Masset is a most wonderful old burying place. The graves are made thus. Two solid cedar tree trunks were sunk in the earth about 14 ft. apart. This was bridged with heavy slabs of wood about 6 or 8 ft. from the ground. There the coffin rested. These must be very old, for in every instance of the six or eight still standing, great spruce trees are growing from the top. You can see that they have seeded themselves in the pithy top of the cedar posts; here they have grown, throwing strong roots down to the earth through the centre of the cedar trunks and bursting them apart. Some tribes cremate their dead, and the widow is compelled to carry the charred bones of her dead husband round with her for one year. Another common practice is to place the coffin in the treetops, lopping off all the under branches and binding them securely to the topmost boughs; here they will remain for a great number of years. And it is customary to bring blankets and anything particularly prized by the deceased nearby.

I will never forget a grave I saw many years ago at Ucluelet on the West coast of Vancouver Island. It was that of a young woman. The coffin was a box about the size of an ordinary trunk, for they double the dead into a sitting posture. A scarlet blanket was bound about the box, and over that again was spread a gay patchwork quilt. This coffin was placed in a hollow cedar tree trunk. Gay beads were spread about, a hanging lamp and other personal treasures of the deceased. The wood was dark and sombre, but somehow a stray sunbeam had filtered through a rift in the hollow tree, lighting up the patchwork quilt and the gay trinkets. The effect in that dark wood was both beautiful and weird. It is customary there when a beloved one dies to burn his house down that it may go to the spirit world for his shelter there.

In No. 64 you will see a burying ground in the woods of Alert Bay, taken some years ago. That thunderbird with spread wings is also from an Alert Bay cemetery. In the same place are many strange paintings, carvings, representations of the copper chests of drawers and other furniture put on graves.

Hazelton possesses a very quaint graveyard. It is on the bluff behind the town and the view from there is magnificent. The dead are buried in the ground and perfect little miniature houses are built over them, having chimneys, windows, doors, etc. You will see all the treasures of the dead: clothes, sewing machines, children's toys, women's hair, warrior's weapons, dishes, boots, hats and if possible a photo of the deceased (though this was only in a case of a young person as the old ones do not like pictures of themselves). This cemetery is divided into little streets. The little houses of the dead are gaily painted. No two are alike in colour and design. They also have little gardens round them.

Picture No. [?] represents the graves at Hagglegate. Here they are quite near to the village, straggling along at the top of the bank. The mountain behind is the glorious Rocher de Boule.

At Kitseukla they also build houses of the dead in front of the village. In looking through the window of one of these houses, one gets a considerable shock to meet the pallid gaze of a young man sitting within. After you have become accustomed to the gloom of the interior, you see it is a wooden effigy, dressed in real clothes and hat; he is seated in a chair, the one hand on his rifle and, in the other outstretched palm, five bullets. The face is very ghastly. This young fellow committed a murder. The police tracked him down, but when he saw he was cornered, he shot himself rather than be taken. Some tribes used to keep bodies of dead personages in their dwelling house for months.

This little story was told to me by Dr. Newcombe. He was travelling among the Indians, and on one occasion was put into a room to sleep, the chief ornament of which was a fine new coffin. On inquiring, he found that his host, although in excellent health, had acquired it against the day of his death. He had previously possessed another, but upon the death of his great friend, he had presented him his own coffin as the highest honour he could bestow. His nephews, therefore, gave him this second one, and now his great worry was that he was growing very stout and he feared he would outgrow it. He used to get in now and again to reassure himself.

There is one other village I would like to mention before I close; that is Guyasdoms. Guyasdoms is about eighteen miles from Alert Bay. I went there through the kindness of Mr. Halliday, the Indian agent at Alert Bay, who was going on a business trip up the Kinkom Inlet. I took a young Indian girl with me, and when we were deposited on the beach and the launch went its way, we were the only living creatures in the place with the exception of a poor half-mad dog who had been forsaken and gone wild. The Indians were all off at the fishing [grounds]. Not a soul remained. Guyasdoms differs absolutely from Alert Bay in that the latter is a show village where all the tourist boats call and the Indians cater to the tourist trade and to the spectacular. Guyasdoms, on the other hand, lies off the beaten track in one of the old-time original villages, unchanged by fashion and civilization. It is large, extending along the waterfront above three beautiful beaches of white shell and pebbles. These three beaches are divided by points so that you do not see the entire village as you approach and are surprised to find how large it is upon investigation.

Among my pictures will be seen two specimens of the houses of Guyasdoms, Nos. 93 and 7, and truly dignified dwellings they are (from the front); all the grandeur of their buildings is "forrard." The back and sides are formed of any old thing in the shape of planks, logs, bark or matting of any old size and shape. There are no windows, sufficient light and air filtering in through the gaps and cracks, and the large smoke[hole] in the roof. This is an adjustable flap that can be regulated according to the wind. But the fronts of these houses are truly imposing. No. 1 was formed of solid hand-hewn cedar planks some inches in thickness, and the posts and beams are enormous across the top, one solid cedar beam carved with the moon totem in the centre and the mythical sea serpent each end. No. 93 is one of the most dignified paganish mansions I have ever seen. The door in the centre is formed through the totem pole, a large whale with a little man astride his back and a flying thunderbird above. The entrance is through a heavy door in the whale's mouth. A flight of steps formed of solid logs banked with clay descends to the beach. It is so primitive, so heathenish, and withal so dignified. The people having been absent some months, the place had become completely overgrown with nettles; they were 8 ft. high, towering above our heads and cruelly stinging our ears and foreheads as we battled our way through them. To make matters worse, in front of the houses were wide plank walks hidden by the nettles and covered with large white slugs; these wretched creatures made it so slimy that we frequently took headlong plunges into the nettle beds. Imagine again the shock of picking oneself out of this predicament to come face to face with that [blank in text] with its outstretched arms and diabolical face. But there she stands, towering above the nettles. We reached a little above her knee as we stood beside her. She is D'Sonoqua, or wood spirit.

What a weird night that was at Guyasdoms. We slept on the floor of the old mission house. How absolutely lonely; the windows had no blinds, and tall trees with coffins bound to their topmost branches rocked their gruesome burdens all night, the wind moaned, the forsaken dog uttered his plaintive howl, the rats were much in evidence and the bed vastly uncomfortable. My little Indian companion alternately whispered of the ghosts and snored loudly. How small one feels in these great vastnesses of nature, alone.

And so I have gone about my work making this collection of Indian totems and I am not through yet. What I have done, I have done alone and single-handed. I have been backed by neither companies nor individuals. I have borne my own expenses and done my own work. My sole protector and companion has been the old faithful dog. I am a Canadian born and bred. I glory in our wonderful West and I [would] like to leave behind me some of the relics of its first primitive greatness. These things should be to us Canadians what the ancient Britons' relics are to the English. Only a few more years and they will be gone forever into silent nothingness, and I would gather my collection together before they are forever past.

[Written on page 51 verso of manuscript] There are many difficulties to be met and overcome in the work, but two things help and spur me on. The love I have for the simple gentle folk and the desire to leave in this, my own Province of British Columbia, a collection of the things that she need not be ashamed of when they have ceased to exist.

AUTOBIOGRAPHY

I was born in Victoria, B.C., in 1871. On leaving high school, I went to San Francisco as a student at the Mark Hopkins School of Art and spent three years there. I returned to Victoria and taught children's classes and saved up for a trip to Europe.

I attended the Westminster School of Art in London. But after the free, wild life of the West, London wilted the very life out of me, so I went down to Cornwall and studied in the open, also to the Bushey studios. Returning again to Westminster School, I broke down completely, wrestled three years with desperate illness, then returned to Canada and started all over again, working and saving, this time with Paris in view. Teaching in Vancouver and very successful with children's classes, I was asked to teach in the art club and made a complete failure, their complaint being "that I could not realize that they were just amusing themselves and tried to make the ladies work in earnest." So they dismissed me. I was glad.

In 1911 I went to Paris with a letter of introduction to a modern painter of Scotch birth, Harry Gibb. This man opened my eyes to the joyousness of the new school. At that time he was being bitterly criticized.

By his advice, I became a student at the Académie Colarossi, Paris. I could not stand the airlessness of the life rooms for long, the doctors stating, as they had done in London, that "there was something about these big cities that these Canadians from their big spaces couldn't stand, it was like putting a pine tree in a pot." So I left Paris and joined outdoor classes under Mr. Gibb, who was then in Brittany. When my money was spent I returned to Canada, but they hated and ridiculed my work. My first exhibition here they dishonoured my work, putting it behind things, under shelves or on the ceiling. My friends begged me to go back to my old way of painting, but I had tasted the joys of a bigger way. It would have been impossible had I wanted to, which I did not. Whenever I could afford it I went up North, among the Indians and the woods, and forgot all about everything in the joy of those lonely, wonderful places. I decided to try and make as good a representative collection of those old villages and wonderful totem poles as I could, for the love of the people and the love of the places and the love of the art; whether anybody liked them or not I did not care a bean.

I painted them to please myself in my own way, but I also stuck rigidly to the facts because I knew I was painting history. The war came (1914). I had a living to make. Of course, nobody wanted to buy my pictures. I'd never tried to paint to please them anyway, so I did horrible things like taking boarders to make a living, and the very little time I had for painting I tried to paint in the despised, adorable joyous modern way. The last two years I have taken up ... pottery, adapting and utilizing my Indian designs for it. A much pleasanter livelihood than catering to people's appetites.

A PEOPLE'S GALLERY

You have been invited here tonight to view this exhibition on the walls that a suggestion may be put before you for your consideration. Viz. the converting of these rooms into a small picture gallery for the use of the people of Victoria.

The Arts and Crafts, a society of long standing in Victoria, has rendered valuable service to Victoria by providing a yearly exhibition and also holding sketch classes. But there would seem now to be a furthering need. One that touches all classes, all nationalities, all colours.

The proposed art gallery would have a different objective and would in no way interfere or overlay the undertakings of the other society. It would be a place for those who do know something about art, but would also be a place for those who do not and maybe want to. A place for the spirit of art to grow in.

Situated on the very edge of Beacon Hill Park. Possibly linked to the park in name and called the Beacon Hill Galleries. (A people's gallery in a people's park.) A warm, quiet nook to drop into on those dull winter days when no band plays. A place one could sit and rest and look at pictures in, which would be changed every few weeks. Pictures of all types: conservative, progressive, oriental, children's. Let the gallery be opened on Saturday mornings specially for the children. On Sundays let it be free for all. On weekdays a small fee might be charged to help with running expenses.

In summer the visitors who so frequently ask, "Is there no picture gallery in Victoria?" could take it in, for the sightseeing buses pass the very door. These visitors would also help on the expense of upkeep.

It would be of benefit to the artists of Victoria by getting their work known. There are also young Orientals in our midst with their fine inborn sensitiveness to art, and no encouragement whatever to go ahead. Boys who have asked for membership to the existing club in Victoria and been refused.

You would be surprised, as I have been, at the art love popping out of odd corners. The other day a negro came to my house, delivering coal. I came to the door with my hands full of paintbrushes. As I signed his book, he said, "Gee! I envy you." "Why?" I asked. "Because I own a monkey?" For I had heard him joking with the monkey below. "No," he replied. "Because you can paint. Gee I'd love to go out to nature and paint." Another day I came to my studio to find two men, hands shading their eyes and noses flattened against the big north window. I flew to the door, angry as a wildcat. "What do you what?" I asked. "Don't you know it's rude to peer into people's windows?" The man, a baker, drew back. "I'm sorry," he said. "I did not realize it was rude. I do admire those pictures and this other man likes pictures too." So I said I'd show him some.

As for the old vegetable Chinaman, he never misses an opportunity to look in and show real interest. When he went home to China, I gave him a picture to take to his wife. He was much pleased; he had three to choose from and unerringly chose the best. So there you are. Could any of those there go to the annual Victoria exhibition and feel comfortable?

One of the loveliest things about the Louvre in Paris is Sunday, the "people's day." Then you see soldiers and peasants, workmen and butchers' boys also, with their empty wooden trays and their blue blouses, doubtless pinching a few moments of their employers' time to reverently peep in at the nation's art treasures.

We may not have here Old Masters to study and enjoy, but who knows what future masters may be hidden away among the rising generation in our very midst, who might be helped and encouraged by this little gallery. We already have a splendid selection of art books in both our libraries, and short talks in the gallery would be very helpful too and start our young folk a long way on the road to thinking on these things.

Now, of course, there's that pestiferous money business that butts into everything. This is no job for the city fathers and the overburdened taxpayer. At present the poor things have more than they can bear. But it is the time of all others that the *people* need a little happiness of art in their lives, to lead them for brief spells from the bread and butter problems.

It would not take very much money. To start simply and happily we don't need a stone edifice and liveried attendants, rooms full of priceless pictures and the wrangle and worry of trying to be able to boast that we have the most magnificent gallery in all Canada. We want to grow and to learn to see the real beauty in those things close about us, to learn to express them in paint or to see them so expressed and to understand.

It is to the many clubs and societies of Victoria that I would make my appeal for help, and particularly to the women's clubs as well as to interested individuals. Not asking any of you to give a lot, but many of you to each give a little, and all of you, if the idea appeals to you, to give it moral support and mothering.

We have lots of material here to draw from, and I've a notion perhaps artists from other places might lend us a parcel of sketches sometimes. We'll round up the artists we know and dig out unknown ones; we won't worry about gold and silver frames in our shows but try to get down to understanding and expressing the real things right here all about us.

I have thought this idea over in a careful practical way for a considerable time, and it seems to me workable. Now I turn it over to you for your weighing, suggesting that it might be given a three-month trial. It would take Victoria quite that time to realize its existence, slow catchers-on we are.

UCLUELET

[...] No one disturbed the Indian dead. Their place was a small, half-cleared spot, a little off from the village and at the edge of the forest. When an Indian died no time was lost in hurrying the body away. While death was approaching a box was got ready. Sometimes, if they owned one, a trunk was used. The body did not lie straight and stark in the box. It was folded up; often it

was placed in the box before it really was a corpse. When life had quite gone, the box was closed, some boards were broken from the side wall of the house, and it was taken away through the hole which was later mended so that the spirit should not remember how it got out and come bothering back.

The people never went to the dead's place except to carry another dead body there and then they would hurry back to make dreadful mourning howls in the village.

One day I went to the place of the dead to sketch. It was creepy. At first I did not know whether I could bear it or not. Bones lay about—human bones—skulls, staring from their eye hollows, stuck out from under the bracken, ribs and thigh bones lay among the roots of the trees where coffin boxes had split. Many "dead-boxes" were bound to the high branches of the pines. The lower limbs of the trees were chopped away. Sometimes a Hudson's Bay blanket would be bound around the box, and flapped in the wind as the tree rocked the box. Up there in the keen air the body disintegrated quickly. The sun and the rain rotted the ropes that bound the box to the tree. They broke and the bones were flung to earth where greenery soon hid them.

It was beautiful how the sea air and sun hurried to help the corpses through their horror. The poor, frail boxes could not keep the elements out; they were quick to make the bones clean and white.

Sometimes Indians used the hollow boles of ancient cedar trees as grave holes, though life was still racing through the cedar's outer shell.

In one of these hollow trees the Indians had lately buried a young woman. They had put her in a trunk. There was a scarlet blanket over the top. Scattered upon that were some beads and bracelets. There was a brass lamp and her clothes too. The sun streamed in through the split in the side of the tree and sparkled on her dear things. This young woman lay in the very heart of the living cedar tree. As I stood looking, suddenly twigs crackled and bracken shivered behind me. My throat went dry and my forehead wet — but it was only Indian dogs.

Up behind Toxis the forest climbed a steep hill and here in the woods was one lonely grave, that of "our only professed Christian Indian," according to the Missionaries. The Missionaries had coffined him tight and carried him up the new-made trail with great difficulty. They put him into the earth among the roots of the trees, away from all his people, away from the rain and the sun and the wind which he had loved and which would have rushed to help his body melt quickly into the dust to make earth richer because this man had lived.

FRIENDS

[...] On Sunday, Louisa opened the chest in my room and dressed her family. Then we all went to church.

The Missionary and his sister shook hands with us and asked us to tea the next day. Louisa could not go, but I went.

The Missionary said, "It is good for the Indians to have a white person stay in their homes; we are at a very difficult stage with them — this passing from old ways into new. I tell you

savages were easier to handle than these half-civilized people...
in fact it is impossible...I have sent my wife and children
south...."

"Is the school here not good?"

"I can't have my children mix with the Indians."

A long pause, then, "I want to ask you to try to use your
influence with Louisa and her husband to send their boys to the
Industrial boarding-school for Indians. Will you do so?" asked
the Parson.

"No."

The Missionary's eyes and his sister's glared at me through
their spectacles like fish eyes.

"Why will you not?"

"In Louisa's house now there is an adopted child, a lazy,
detestable boy, the product of an Indian Industrial School,
ashamed of his Indian heritage. All Louisa's large family of children are dead, all but these two boys, and they are not robust.
Louisa knows how to look after them—there is a school in the
village. She can send them there and own and mother them
during their short lives. Why should she give up her boys?"

"But the advantages?"

"And the disadvantages!"

Louisa and I sat by the kitchen stove. Joe, her younger son, had
thrown himself across her lap to lull a toothache; his cheeks
were thin and too pink. Louisa said, "The Missionary wants us
to send our boys away to school."

"Are you going to?"

"—Maybe Jimmy by and by—he is strong and very bright,
not this one—."

"I never saw brighter eyes than your Joe has."

Louisa clutched the boy tight. "Don't tell me that. They say shiny eyes and pink cheeks mean—...If he was your boy, Em'ly, would you send him away to school?"

"NO."

MARTHA'S JOEY

One day our father and his three little girls were going over James Bay Bridge in Victoria. We met a jolly-faced old Indian woman with a little fair-haired white boy about as old as I was.

Father said, "Hello Joey!" and to the woman he said, "How are you getting on, Martha?"

Father had given each of us a big flat chocolate in silver papers done up like a dollar piece. We were saving them to eat when we got home.

Father said, "Who will give her chocolate to Joey?"

We were all willing. Father took mine because I was the smallest and the greediest of his little girls.

The boy took it from my hand shyly, but Martha beamed so wide all over me that I felt very generous.

After we had passed on I said, "Father, who is Joey?"

"Joey," said my father, "was left when he was a tiny baby at Indian Martha's house. One very dark stormy night a man and woman knocked at her door. They asked if she would take the child in out of the wet, while they went on an errand. They would soon be back, they said, but they never came again, though Martha went on expecting them and caring for the child. She washed the fine clothes he had been dressed in and took them to the priest; but nobody could find out anything about the couple who had forsaken the baby.

"Martha had no children and she got to love the boy very much. She dressed him in Indian clothes and took him for her own. She called him Joey."

I often thought about what Father had told us about Joey.

One day Mother said I could go with her, and we went to a little hut in a green field where somebody's cows grazed. That was where Martha lived.

We knocked at the door but there was no answer. As we stood there we could hear someone inside the house crying and crying. Mother opened the door and we went in.

Martha was sitting on the floor. Her hair was sticking out wildly, and her face was all swollen with crying. Things were thrown about the floor as if she did not care about anything any more. She could only sit swaying back and forth crying out, "Joey—my Joey—my Joey—."

Mother put some nice things on the floor beside her, but she did not look at them. She just went on crying and moaning.

Mother bent over Martha and stroked her shoulder; but it was no good saying anything, she was sobbing too hard to hear. I don't think she even knew we were there. The cat came and cried and begged for food. The house was cold.

Mother was crying a little when we came away.

"Is Joey dead, Mother?"

"No, the priests have taken him from Martha and sent him away to school."

"Why couldn't he stay with Martha and go to school like other Indian boys?"

"Joey is not an Indian; he is a white boy. Martha is not his mother."

"But Joey's mother did not want him; she gave him away to Martha and that made him her boy. He's hers. It's beastly of the priest to steal him from Martha."

Martha cried till she had no more tears and then she died.

PART THREE

Page 215: Photo inscribed on the back: "Lady June [the dog] and Emily Carr wish Ira Dilworth a Merry Christmas, 1942." B.C. Archives I-51568

The letters to Emily Carr from Sophie Frank are few, but they indicate that a continuing if intermittent contact between the two women was kept up over several decades. The letter from Jimmy Frank, Sophie's husband, written at Christmas the year Sophie died, speaks to the importance of this friendship, and the recognition accorded it.

The two women met in Vancouver shortly after Carr went there to live in 1906. Carr would often cross Burrard Inlet to visit with Sophie Frank at her house on the reserve, which in those days was called Squamish Mission. She followed her friend's travails with her sickly children; when one infant, whom Sophie named after Emily, died, Carr purchased a gravestone for her. And when Carr left the city to return to Victoria, the friendship continued.

Although one of Sophie Frank's letters has been published, the record has continued to construe her as but an acquaintance of Carr's, an illiterate "funny" English speaker, who was not so much a friend of Carr's as a figment of her imagination; a prop for her painterly persona. The more generous view has described Sophie as a kindly protegé of Carr's. However, with these letters come Sophie Frank's voice and a glimpse into her life. Given that she was the only indigenous artist with whom Carr had an ongoing relationship, Sophie was a significant figure in her life and almost certainly a source and probably a mentor. Still, she remains a shadowy figure. Little is known about her beyond the Native community, and what is known comes mainly from Emily Carr. Sophie Frank's background and family, as well as her reputation as a basket maker, have only begun to be investigated.

The correspondence between Emily Carr and Ira Dilworth constitutes a large file, several folders thick. Although originally from Victoria, Dilworth was living in Vancouver, where he was regional director for the Canadian Broadcasting Corporation, when he met Carr. The distance necessitated communication by letter, and Carr was an assiduous correspondent. More than two hundred missives poured forth from her. Dilworth's responses were not nearly so effusive, but he reciprocated and was ever attentive, communicating with Carr by phone (occasionally) and by wire, and on special occasions sending flowers. (So often at one point that Carr wrote him to suggest he was being extravagant.)

Early on in their friendship, and perhaps occasioned by the stories of her childhood that she was preparing for *The Book of Small*, Carr began adopting the voice and character of her childhood self, whom she dubbed Small, when writing to Dilworth. Often Small and Emily would write together in the same letter, Small addressing him as her "dear Guardian," and Emily calling him "Eye." In September 1942, talking about Small, Carr writes:

> I look up at your picture and wonder how you would have fathered Small. I've never had any fatherly feelings towards you; as you know I adored Father as a tot and then hated him. I've only known a very small brother's love. The love I gave you certainly was not the type I gave to my sweetheart, a love that expects a whole heap back. It was a better love than any of these; its foundation was in lovely things.... When Sophie

called me "friend" it was friend in the true sense of the word. When someone says my friend Mrs. Smith it means nothing; friend can be a deep word or have no meaning at all. Perhaps the kind of meaning my love has for you and I'd like yours to have for me is comrade; comradeship seems so expansive somehow, a turning into things together.

The affection and closeness between Carr and Dilworth are palpable, and on a few occasions she speaks of her love for him. In a letter in September 1944, she trails off at the end with this message, and without her usual fond farewells:

Beloved old Ira, how I have loved you for that very quality [his appreciation of music, poetry and painting]. I have only done you one wrong, been possibly only one way unfair, I have possibly loved you too deeply. I can only beg—forgive me—

And in the autumn of 1944, a few months before she died, she writes:

I've been so proud of your friendship, and my love for you has been very deep and very sincere. I can't imagine life since I had to give up painting (tramping round free) without [it].

Ira Dilworth was Emily Carr's editor, confidant and the last great love in her life. Indeed, she wrote more frequently to him in her last years than she did in her journal, sharing her thoughts, her memories and her obsessions with him. She does not often write about art, but she talks about writing and the reviews of her books. She also writes about her sister Alice, and Alice's descent into blindness. But the letters also chronicle the story of Emily Carr's own decline, the slow narrowing of her world, as she prepared for her own departure.

LETTERS FROM SOPHIE AND JIMMY FRANK
TO EMILY CARR

Squamish Mission
North Vancouver
March 19th, 1915

My dear Emily,

With great pleasure I write you these few lines in answer to your letter. I am well and Frank too but he is just as bad in drinking. I just begin to feel alright and good of heart and then he drinks and makes me down-hearted again. I can't get cheerful for I can't make him good.

I am very tired of selling baskets. I have lots though but no one cares much for them. All say that they have no money. Frank has not been working lately. He has been home always so I can't make much alone. I buy all our food. I love the warm weather that is coming. I have not been working in my garden for I am in Vancouver every day trying to sell baskets.

Yes it is too bad about the war. I feel sorry for the poor ladies that tell me of their husbands who are gone.

My father is well and he does feel sorry for Alexander. I was to Squamish River to see my sister to see her little new baby and her only little girl is not well at all.

Sarah is well and Mary Annie too. She is gone to her home in Sechelt to get dried herring. Granny is well too. She is at Squamish River at present.

My father is getting old and foolish now. He comes to town and spends his money in drinking and every way foolishly. I never see him; he does not come to see me.

Well, I will close with my best love and wishing you a Happy Easter when it comes. I hope you will enjoy the time.

Your ever loving friend

Sophie Frank

August 6th, 1915

North Vancouver, B.C.

My dear Emily,

I would only be too glad if I could go, but I am not feeling well. The waves make me sick. So you must not feel sorry about it.

I would bring the mat or send it but because the lady is not sure to buy it. The Indians are not like the white people; the lady is not allowed to go alone any place.

Don't be too sorry about it though. I can't help it. I'd like to go but I don't like the sea voyage.

Your dear friend,

Sophie Frank

North Vancouver

March 1st, 1929

My dear Emily,

I received your letter of the 4th and we was sure glad to hear from you once again.

We feel sorry you was sick with the flu and I hope you will be strong in the near future. As for ourselves, we are well at present.

Yes, I am selling and making baskets for my living. Frank can't work now. He got odd jobs once in a while. Well, my father is old now and his house got burned about a month ago. I feel bad for I cannot get to go and see him up Squamish Valley.

I must come to a close and hope you be alright soon.

Your friend,
Sophie Frank

Squamish P.O.
British Columbia
December 8th, 1939

My dear friend,

I guess you thought I forgot you but I still think of you. So I just thought I would drop a line and let you know how I'm getting along. I am quite well at present as I still staying at Squamish as I left North Vancouver after my wife died.

I'm keeping away from drink. I'm better off here. I'm having a hard time but I get along. I'll be in North Van before Xmas.

I cannot forget my wife. It's pretty hard and sure is very lonesome without her. I hope you are well and please answer.

Jimmy Frank

P.S. Wishing you a very happy Xmas and happy New Year.

LETTERS FROM EMILY CARR
TO IRA DILWORTH

December 14th, 1941
Sunday Morn, 3:30 A.M.

Dearest Guardian,

How wonderful our Birthday party was! I was terrifically happy. When Emily saw all those people she thought she was going to get the jitters. But I didn't, though. I can't say what I might have felt if I hadn't seen my dear Guardian almost first thing. It was so comfortable to see my home right there.

Wasn't everybody *lovely*? And the dear flowers and the letters. And best of all that lovely kiss you gave Small in front of them all when you finished reading. (Better than the whole bottle of Emily's heart pills.) I am so grateful to you for being there; it meant everything strong to Emily and to me.

Your Small

Noon Sunday

Cod. P.S. from Emily

Would you expect the child to sleep all through the night after such a day? She didn't, but she's OK and gloating over her room full of flowers. They are fresh and new as the morning. They are so lovely.

P.S.er The letters were marvellous. You shall read them. *Do tell me* what to do about the *enormous* ones. Do I write to Canadian Press (Where and how?) the Mayor? The Women's Canadian Club? How about the Lieutenant Governor? And the Premier. Surely not?? The Indian Agents, yes, of course. There are twenty letters in the mail.

P.S.est I am resting in my poems today. Small loves them. Snooze poems, snooze poems, that's the order today.

Cod. P.S.est I've thought so often of that Indian boy looking at Sophie.

December 23rd, 1941

Dear Ira,

A happy peaceful Christmas day at peace in your own self. Even if the big world yowls we each have a little world of our own in our own hearts to rule over and be happy in.

I am glad you left Jane tonight. I like to have her and I like to know I have not added to your already over-heavy burden by landing that whirligig on you. I always loved naughty kids better than goody-goodies, Martyn (in the biog) *almost* made me quaver with love for him once when the "Elder" had told me I was the Black Sheep of the family and the only one that my mother felt anxiety over on her deathbed. It made me feel bad, but Martyn said, "Well, if you were *the bad one,* you may be sure your mother loved you just a *little* more than the others." That was such a comfort to me — I'd never thought of such a thing, only of Mother's being so disappointed in her bad child.

The Biog is my Christmas present to you. Accept as your *very own* with my love. It is far from finished. There is a lot more in London and then back to Canada yet to be done but you told me *not to hurry* it so I have been deliberate and tried to dig. I have written it for Canadian Art and for you. Its first writing was superficial — afraid to let go and show myself. A very dull document. I utterly *ignored* that M.S. in writing this. The only thing I bothered to follow was the headings. I had decided in the first edition what places and people I was going to write about and I have done so—parts may seem to you superfluous—cut out if so. Parts I may want to rewrite yet again. But I want to get it complete while my wits are clear and before the effort becomes impossible. You know how we *postpone* things. Two sections "St Paul's" and "Westminster Abbey" you already have. I have made *no* duplicate copies of any of it and am destroying the old original as I write this. Having lost my confounded glasses has prevented my going over it for the 2000th time. There are doubtless many bad things that I can refine and simplify after it is once together. If you ever want to publish it you could "edit" without me. I don't think there is anything for relations to kick at. The Boultbee woman was very fond of her aunts (except me) and thought them saints. (Me a devil.) But Mrs. Boultbee's mother had seen enough of the Elder's domineering and autocratic rule over we younger children to *absolutely forbid* the Elder to lift a finger to her children. The nieces *only saw* her soft side. She was older and kinder then than when we were young.

Don't give old Biog thought now. You have all the thinking to do your head has room for. It makes me happy to give it into your keeping as done. I'm such a muddle-bag and loser.

God bless you and rest you and give you peaceful quiet in your heart. No matter what may stir itself with 1942. Small says "Give over Emily! I want my Guardian's eye" so

Love from Emily

Beloved Guardian Ira,

Here's a hug for Xmas and please "Tossed" is my Xmas present to you. See me in it as you see Emily in Juice. I'll sing Spring songs to you out of "Tossed." Others may not hear them—you will and you'll try to shut me in the "Book of Small" too, but don't expect me to stay put in a frame or between the covers. I'm too kicky for that. Fold your arms across your front hard; maybe then I'll keep still and stay put a few moments.

Always your loving Small

February 15th, 1942
Sunday, 7 P.M.

Dear Ira,

Oh! Today's been just that, no more no less. No answers to my ad and Phyllis gone, poor little girl. I was mad with her at 8:30, resigned at 9:30, weepy at noon. Her last job was to (voluntarily) when she was entitled to be beginning [departure] preparations on her own, run for the torch and help me with the intricate job of rewiring and reconstructing my front doorbell. We did it. I turned it inside out with its innards exposed but its ring restored. It will be easier next time as we won't have to rip its inwardness out. I've had an ad in but only a buxom Scotch hussy who expected remuneration according to her size and the family she'd raised and who also had no use for "critters" meaning my menagerie. I did not yearn towards her. A[lice] is so difficult when I am alone; wants to do all the impossibles that she *can't* do and *won't heed* the things she can, she is not so deaf but she lets herself slump into a far-offness. Unless you are amusing her, she simply seals up her senses and you could bellow your tongue off its pivot. I finished Mr. Clarke's bear and have the pictures all crated ready to be called for tomorrow. Did it alone after Phyllis left! Very proud of me I am. Mending doorbells, crating and a long afternoon rest have meant not much accomplished today. News is not nice today is it. I got tired of the "temporary" business. "Temporarily lost" they always say.

How was the lecture last evening? I was with you all the time. Me and Small. Alice had a birthday party for two of her Hennell boys, a very nice dinner, just the four of us. They are very nice lads and *very nice* to her. Heavens she did enough for them in their childhood, but people don't always remember. You've moved. I tuned for Sanctuary, stupid of me to forget change of time, will have to postpone beauty sleep but am so glad it is later not earlier or I should have missed it.

This morning I was reading more of Lawren's letters. There's a tremendous pile and they are very fine. I hardly realized what they meant to my work in the transition stage. *How* he helped me. Rereading them gives me further illumination. What he tells me of his what he says of mine. He *is* a fine man. They are such warm friendly help. I was so far off from all the workers so totally on my own and rather bewildered. I had been through a period somewhere around 15 years dormant all the art smashed out of me flat. There are a few letters of Bess's too, warm loving letters and some from Fred. I am enclosing one about his Walt Whitman book I think may interest you. Of course they (Lawren, Bess and Fred) claimed W.W. was a theosophist pure and simple whether he called himself that or not. I am sorting the letters over. Any that have anything personal any hints which are now clear to me though they were not at the time (as to his personal unhappiness) things I see now but could not then, these I am burning. Nothing really in them but it seems fairer to him. The work letters I shall still keep, they would be of no interest to any one but a worker or a seeker like yourself. They throw light on Lawren's work and on my own too. I think I shall cash [cache] them in "the box" when sorted. Someday you might to be interested to read them? Or bored? You could even let Lawren look over them and ask if you might. People who did not understand or love these things would think it stupid stuff and I'd rather they were burned than that. There was a letter, very happy following immediately on the bust-up. It is rather pitiful. I guess both went through a bit of Hell, probably the whole thing was just unavoidable and right, sometimes our judgements are so very petty and small. Oh how little we are! How we splash around pretending we are whales and are really tadpoles.

I found something I had forgotten viz. Lawren tried to persuade me to write a biog. Practically the thing I *am* doing. I remember jeering and saying, "Who'd want to read it?" and "What had *I* to write about?" and dismissed it from my thoughts. Maybe it did not register then; maybe it sowed the idea; I don't know. I thought it was really because Eric Brown asked me to, said if I wouldn't someone else would. I was amazed to see in these old letters. It was just the type of thing he suggested. I told you I felt hurt when I suggested a year or two ago. I sent it to him to crit the art part and he did not answer. I felt he was indifferent. If it's readable when finished suppose you let him read it? In view of those old letters I feel I ought to, if he is interested, of course. As Bess is his now, I s'pose she'd have to be included. Well I so reduced the parts that would make me squirm and feel silly I don't guess I'd mind. What do you think about it? I don't think I've left myself too naked. I couldn't bear the whole public and I'd hate the ridicule of *my own* relatives. Only one of my nieces commented on Klee Wyck, her comment (Mrs. Boultbee) "that she'd only read a few pages, it was *too heavy* for her to hold in bed." She's always in bed for something, potters in and out of hospitals like the cuckoo in a clock. Too much money to spend on her fads. A great niece or two have mildly commented on K.W. However, one buxom farm girl, Lillian Nicholles's daughter wrote me a short *real* letter, warm, badly worded and genuine. Alice sent the Boultbee woman a copy. I did not. When I was poor and starting studio in Vancouver she was a beautiful and popular bride was very beastly to me so I always have given her a wide berth. She adores Alice. She has always been mean and rude over my work (painting) and is a hypocrite like her pa was.

This brings me, Ira, to something I think I should be frank with my trustees in. Neither of you knows how I stand financially. Neither of you likes to ask but in arranging for the trust you wonder. So I'll try and tell you what my income is though it is a queer precarious affair and I often don't know myself.

My one sure income is a small house in Fairfield I traded my apartment for, rents for $25 per month. I have a few government bonds paying 2 or 2 ½ percent interest (around $10 or $12 a month I s'pose) and (this is a pill) Mrs. Boultbee gives Alice and I, Alice $35 per month, me $15. I hate taking it from her when I feel I don't trust her. It happened this way:—Her husband left her *very* rich — Braelorn Mines. Well, years back she knew Lizzie and Alice had not very much and she gave them $15 a month each to spend on their gardens and little things. I did not speak to her for years; she told some lies and made trouble for me in Vancouver. Well when Lizzie died she came over to weep and to comfort Alice. I made up with Mrs. B and she asked me to accept as *a goodwill gesture* the $15 per month she used to send Lizzie. I was terribly hard up at the time and to refuse would have upset the whole cartload of kiss and make up. Money meant nothing to her so I took it, which makes my income round fifty dollars per month. I have the upkeep and taxes of the Fairfield house, pay $15 per month to Alice for rent and $20 to a maid. But as you know I make a sale now and then, have been very lucky and there is Klee Wyck. These extras go out into the bank to draw from because the $50 won't stretch when I keep a maid. With my rental for my flat and Una's and her bonds Alice gets about $50 too. She owns her house. I have very seriously considered withdrawing from Una's $15 — do you think I should? I expect she has fearful income tax and she spends her life running after cures, in and out of hospital; she hospitals for everything. She is very generous to her family, they are all poor. But if I did she would probably rake up all the old fuss and if I don't I guess she thinks I'm rolling in wealth now K.W. has sold well. There that's me and my pocket. Mr. Lawson our guardian was honest as the day but *no investor.* Father left us comfortable and the old estate all clear but the "Elder" never could keep in bounds. Between the two we only got a few hundreds out of the old place after everything was eaten up in taxes. If my sisters hadn't helped me that long illness in England would have sent Small to the charity orphanage. How mad Lizzie used to be that my art *was not profitable.* I remember Walter Nicholles coming to see my pictures once. He nearly but not quite bought one. Lizzie said "Let him have them for anything, Millie. You'd be well rid of the stuff for even a dollar or two." (My entire Indian collection.) I felt dreadfully hurt, however, Mr. Nicholles did not want them for even a "dollar or two." Maybe that is why I love *giving* them away now. When people love them, and *I like* the people I want to give them far more than to sell.

Oh what a letter,

Forgive,
Emily

N.B. Your drawing of a heart is simply shocking. You'll have to get someone to give you lessons in heart drawing.

April 6th, 1942
218 St. Andrew's

Dear Ira,

Being all in a moil I write to calm myself. There are times when our sediment is all riled not necessarily dirtying but disturbing us for the moment. Old perplexities, past and present, arguing and shouting across intervening times, feeling disappointments over promises unfulfilled, thoughts that blossomed but didn't fruit, dreamings that woke too soon, aspirations that sank and have lain in the mud bottom, too water-logged to hoist ever again and others spiralling up with fresh bubbles and new longings for being riled.

I've been going over my letters (mostly Lawren's with the exception of Bess's occasional one). I find all my hoarded letters are from men. I was supposed to be a man hater!! He, he! I learned more from men, touched them closer, been touched deeper by them than by women. Queer me. I was always called a baby hater too, yet babies always *came* to me, weren't afraid! It would have hurt me dreadfully if they had been — animals and babies liking me burst me with satisfaction. But the letters. Lawren's are splendid. I don't know which I sent you of them. I would send them to no one else but as you know I have his permission. There is warm friendship and love between you two and I believe that both of you love me deeply; and it is because you have taken upon yourselves the care and the burden of the Trust that I feel you as well as Lawren should know what went into its making. I shall, I think, let you have the letters to browse among. There is repetition, always the insistent kindly push — work, work, always the cheering of my despair and discouragements. The delight that those men over there *believed in me*, had faith in what I was striving for, loved what I loved — Canada and things bigger than just money and glory in Art. Those letters show how weak and faltering I was and how Lawren knew the feel of weakness, the struggle necessary in his own work. Those letters are worth more than my whole Biog. I had hoped to make some quotes from them but there is so much of value, I can't choose. As you read, take out and mark any you feel of special value to be put in the Biog will you? Value to other seekers. You will see how he harps on the Biog idea. Yet I was quite unaware that probably he put the idea into my noodle originally when I decided to write it.

There are a couple of letters also from a German man, Gerhardt Ziegler. Pathetic letters. Read them. Oh the fine stuff in humanity and we let nationality drown it. I think I told you about these two German men, one an architect one an engineer who set out to see the world. One died in Arizona; this one returned a physical wreck. Both were mere boys during the other World War. They came out at a time when the world was still bitter against Germans and everyone who met them in my house said "I am glad I met those fine young men, they make me feel different to all Germany."

Well now you are in Toronto safe and sound, I hope. Winter again I s'pose. I hope you snored clean through your Winnipeg break and feel refreshed. We are calmly restfully dull today.

To quote you, "This is not a letter, only a note."

Love and luck from a loving old woman
And Small

September, 1942
1037 Richardson St.
Thursday Morn

My dear Ira,

Your letter came. What a splendid one! I want to get an answer written so that Alice can post it when she comes as you want Small's clothing back quick. Poor Small's been naked *so long* but at least she has a prompt christening which her sister did not get.

Thank you for that letter my dear. As you said, my *heart* knew. And disgrace or immorality I could not link with your name or with any thought of you. Then when you did not write I feared you might be angered that I had *even mentioned* the hag's scandal to you. But I *had to*; it was in our pact. *Straightness* with each other wasn't it? You could have just as easily have thought wrong of Small by the hints I had given you about a terror in her young life but you didn't. You told me you had already guessed. Honest straight speaking is the *only* way to keep square. Yes, I hope and pray clouds will never come between us, never obscure the beauty of our friendship. I feel this has only *deepened* our faith and loving friendship *of each other.* I was glad when I had told you about the horrid twist in Small's life (the opening of her eyes wrong). When you read "Mother" it seemed the time to do it. So that you'd understand. Most of Small's stories were written before that dirty smudge was laid upon life. What should have been explained to me as holy and beautiful in life. I never had anyone to go to who would have put things in their right light. I had to wait until the slow process of nature herself showed me.

Thank your for telling me about your life. You modest critter. I *am proud* of you. I knew a little from your mother but rather muddled. She has such pride in you. Oh Ira, I was so furious. You see that hag spread it—the dirty lie—broadcast it at the meal table. My own nurse told me and half believed it (though she knew the woman was a dirty-tongued liar). Then that teacher put *her* straight and I talked to Mrs. Clarke who told me she knew too much of your reputation to *credit one word* and she knew the woman to be a scandal monger. Mrs Clarke said she had always wanted to meet you. She delayed going out the day you came to see me so she would have the opportunity. Then afterwards when I told her I would not have that woman in my room again because she had said vile lies about my best friend, she went to the kitchen and gave those women her mind, told them the truth and forbade old O'Horror to go into my room. When the other woman is off duty Mrs. Clarke herself looks after me.

Ira dear, I have no way of burning letters here only the wastebasket, so when you come I'll give it back to you for safe disposition as you see fit. But I am *so glad* you told me of the horrors that had come to you. It did not in the least surprise me. Bless you for your dear honest modesty. I can't, like your mother, take to myself the pride of having *made* and *reared* you but I can glory in the wonderful friendship a man like you has given to make my last years happy. And Ira, I felt proud when you said I'd stood up to champion you like Pearl did. I always feel I knew the real Pearl in person through you, just as you said you knew my mother through Small's book.

Which reminds me, Clarke's watercolour of an asinine English setting (an English fool leading Kate Greenaway ninnies) makes me *absolutely sick*. If I thought our Small would ever be made that I'd thrombose and stroke all over again with a whole lot of new and unexpected demises thrown in. I simply WON'T STAND IT. The other I like in its *green* setting; the wallpaper stripe behind might improve it but I *like* the paddy green better than that crushed blood of before. I love green.

I've rather retrograded the last ten days—(but got on). Oh well, ups and downs one has to expect. I wish I'd been along to see Dr. Trapp's new house. s'pose I never shall now. Guess this thrombosis kiboshed future visits. Nobody wants tissue paper parcels. Stout, untearable, butcher paper is the kind for getting about. But we *must* see Dr. Trapp gets that sketch. You know if the thrombosis had fixed things (which it nearly did) Mr. Gage, Dr. Trapp and those others would not have got what I intended. Dr. Baillie told me frankly (I asked him) I could have another thrombosis and it is likely I wouldn't come off so lucky next time. That's why I want to leave things neat. I am a topsy-turvy by nature you know but I think it's mean to the after-you folks don't you? Hard enough at the best of times, and if you have things in order it's a sure way to live 100,000 years. (Heaven forbid!) Of course, you can have "The Clearing." I was surprised when it came home. My nurse unpacked it and "Emily" went starch and said that man will ask for it, "The Clearing," before I send it back.

Your asters still live. Mrs. Clarke takes special care of them because they are yours. If she wants to tease me she says, "We'll throw those asters out today." Then I bounce and she says, "I've taken special care of them. Well, they're not dead, I just wanted to see you brisk up." She was so strong behind me when I *fought for you.*

The world is beautiful today. I have hopes from intimations you may be along end of the week. What of Jane? Don't be afraid to tell me. I've swallowed the hurt of her not being the comfort I had hoped. I see the common sense of it. Alice will be half here now and I'm supposed to rest first. I s'pose that drat blackout gave a lot of extra to C.B.C.

Come soon

Always your loving, Emily

P.S. P.S. Me too, Small

N.B. Am afraid of your being too easy so enclose some vitriol for you to send Clarke if you see fit.

November 17, 1942

Dear Eye,

I loved your reading as you know I *always do.* Thank you for letting me know O.U.P. [Oxford University Press] sent me two reviews. I don't know if I should send them to you or if they will be a bother because I want them back and things one has to return are a nuisance. Still, I *think* you'd like to see them. I have not read them to Alice yet. I hesitate to do so because I fancy she will a little resent some of the things said of the family — of the religion and my sisters being hard on me, particularly Edith and being unsympathetic towards my *art life.* I think these things would anger Alice. She would think it disloyal. Is it Eye? But it is no good trying to write if you are not honest. It's just sentimental goo. But Alice would like that. I only see Alice every two or three days. We have hardly mentioned The Book of Small. Mr. Clarke told her not to let me read aloud too much, but I do read her a little of Small and Mrs. Wilson has read it to her.

I have never talked to her about my "flop fears." I expect she thinks it *is flop* as up to these two there have been no reviews to read her. Somehow, Eye, I can't talk about Small. Klee Wyck was different. I am fond of both Mrs. Clarke and Mrs. Roy but I never mention Small to them. Nor do they mention the book to me. I keep my copy in a drawer. If anyone *asks* to see her they go to the drawer to get her. Few do ask.

There is one thing makes me glad though. (Nobody but you will understand this.) I had not realized how much of Father there was in the book. Of course, all of her is stories before that brutal telling and the horrible crack-up of Small's lovely world which broke the fond, devoted relationship between us. I was bitterly unforgiving. It must have been dreadfully hurtful to Father. Knowing you Ira chased the bitters out of Small. Small's being able to tell the dearest friend she ever had and that friend's understanding seemed to smooth away the old scar. If I have made people respect and honour Father through The Book of Small perhaps it has in someway atoned for all my years of bitterness.

There is not much of Mother in The Book of Small. I suppose Father was the dominant element in our house at that time. But I loved Mother *best.* I think you will see that in the "Portrait of My Mother" that I gave you. I think perhaps that is the tenderest most loving bit of writing I have ever done. I *wanted* to do it and I am glad I did it at Mount Douglas before my collapse (whether she will ever be published or not I don't know. I'd like people to know my mother. You say she belongs in the biog. There was not anything to make right with Mother like there was with Father. There was only love; no hurt.

The will is all fixed up and squared at last. I was shocked to find how muddled it was. It would have been in a big mess about the ms and not at all as I intended—half you, half Alice. No you 'til Alice's death at all. I explained to Harry that Alice might live ten years yet or more and by that time the royalties of my books might be all worn out. There's not much selling after a book's new is off, I expect? He did not approve of *half in half*; said it would send death-duty nose pokers into it and be bad and be a great trial to Alice. Harry had left Alice, Willie and Lawren in a mix. Our pictures too, so we had to settle that. I have given her now that big canvas in my studio over the table. Lawren put a reserve of $500 on it. It is liable to sell someday being of historic value. It is *hers* any time it sells or to *will* if she wants and where she wants but she is *out* of the other pictures and therefore *cannot will* them back to her nieces. Oh pshaw! Wills! But I am glad it's tidied up. It was worse than no will.

I wonder if you will have to go North? I've been up in a chair doing a little rough type. My head is not too good for work.

How is your help doing? Did Phyllis start her job today? What's the good of asking questions you don't answer? That's nasty! You *are good* to me in your busy life but is the anthology getting anywhere??? Isn't Mrs. Clarke an *awful* writer, *far* worse that you and as bad as me.

There's a door going bang, bang, bang. I long to roam into the hall and *slam* it.

Good night,

Your loving Emily & Small

P.S. If you would prefer nose, mouth or ear, say so. I am adaptable.

c.o.d. Carol wanted to be remembered to you. She is just a little jealous because she's so far off and you nearer. She loves Small but says she can't take the place of Klee Wyck quite with her. Klee Wyck was [her] first love. Bill and Rolf like Small best. Joe sent me a dear little letter and a box of candy which he called a "getting better present." He is a dear little boy. I don't wonder

Carol adores him. She is truly fond of Bill. It is a thoroughly happy marriage but there seems a tremendous link between her and Joe.

February 14th, 1945

Dear Eye,

The child was so pleased with her Valentine. We began the day bleak and thunderous. The night before was a bad one. I felt at my wit's end and came to the conclusion something *must* be done. I could *not* go on. Two years is enough of a sentence so did not feel I was giving the new medicine a show either. Shanks has been unbearable and Alice as obstinate and worrying as possible. She *will* crawl round at night three or four times. Once is OK as the house gets bitter cold before morning but she took to several times and wore herself out and worried me. I felt I hadn't a soul to turn to and I longed to go to Harry; his wife wrote me that morning. She said I know you are one of his friends who will miss him most for there was always a "sincere deep friendship between you two." Then I woke at midnight and everything seemed one too many and I had a bad rest of the night, and started as a huge boo-hoo cry. Shanks had had her dismissal from Thursday (we were going to get a "worker by hour"; this seemed the sort of thing available). Finally I thought of St. Mary's Priory (old James Bay Hotel) where they take old and infirm people in, and Dr. Baillie came this morning and he thinks it quite a good idea. You see Alice is getting worn out and it is not fair. Of course she's furious and hurt but Dr. Baillie will make inquiries. Alice says "You'll hate it." I know I shall but I hated going to Mrs. Clarke's and I hated it while I was there yet I stuck it six months without grumbling and I can do it again. So we are leaving things in abeyance several days. Shanks came through and offered to stay on any odd days 'til I get something. So that's the way it is. They'd both bullied me so for being difficult and I asked Dr. B, "Tell me, is it all my fault?" He said, *"No it was not."* I saw I'd come to the end. I have had it with poor Alice getting up at night and often quite unnecessarily but so obstinate. So you may find me anywhere if you come next week. Me and Small. I'll take her. I hope she will stay close. Yes, Small was round when Lawren was there; but, of course, he did *not* know about her belonging to both of us. Only just I know that. One or two call me Small but that is just from reading the book.

I am glad you enjoyed Hundreds and Thousands. I've written two since. I am *not* surprised that many need rewriting. Next batch will be small only 10–15. I found so many confusing. You are not to press yourself to crit but just read for fun at present. I fully understand. I am only glad you are getting fun out if it for yourself — although I did not know most of it *was* funny. These last two I feel [I'm] getting a little more into my stride. I know many of the others I sent you were too long, not concise enough. I must try and just pick out the core of the thought and wean the extra round it. So many of the things I would write about are already in various M.S. and I don't want to repeat. Suddenly, with the talking, a hundred characters will pop into my head but I must [write] or it eludes me. I write down on any scrap of paper (and lose it generally). Today I got up and had Royal help me put the paint sketches back in my work corner; and I signed *them all.* Last year when I was so ill, I was worried because half were *unsigned.* Now all are done; only some little pieces. "Sky and Sea" I hear is finished, so I must get it before next week. If I go into the "Cripple Priory" I would want to leave the sketches for Willie to crate. Max [Stern] wants them after but he wants them *unframed.* He says he shall frame them anyhow and the wood frame will add so much to the postage but I don't see how *that can be arranged.* I would think I'd better send his letter to Lawren. He is in such close touch [with] the gallery. Max sent me $350 more. Some few odd sales and the balance of the others he says. He has not sold any of the new watercolours because he has not shown them yet. Expects to show them in April. If they are off my chest I can take my writing into the "old" place. You see it is near enough for Alice to walk once a day and alone. I hate the thought of leaving her alone but she loves solitude and her flat, in fact she loves it more and more. She has several neighbour friends. Lillian Martin is sweet and good going to see her. Lady Boultbee has not put in an appearance as yet. I'd like to get something settled before she comes or she'll be bitter and horrid at me being such a care on Alice.

Don't be too sorry for me Eye. It will just be another chapter of life (another Hundred and Thousand). I must finish off "Indefinitely" (Mr. Clarke's house). The sheets of them have got scattered.

Spring *will* come and it *is* nearer home than Mrs. Clarke's. I do love home. Dr. sent in a nurse tonight and after all it is a comfort to feel she's there, an estrangement but a comfort and Max's new cheque made me feel it possible I could. I shall probably keep her a week. She just said, "Do you know where you ought to be? *In hospital.*" I have hospitaled enough for a few weeks. I said, "Oh no, you can't get hospital care now, and it so short of everything and crowded. Even Dr. Baillie said so." She is a nice little nurse, quite understanding. Dr. Baillie is an old dear. He was with me half an hour after he heard I was rotten this A.M., though he had seen me on Saturday. He seemed to take the whole situation in. He's always funny. I was hunting for my hankie, needing it dreadfully, and I said goodness I'm just sick of hunting these silly scraps of hankies in my bed, so I've taken to sheets and *now they're lost* and [then] I found the great one I had for my cold. "That's an 80-cylinder hanky," he laughed. And how wretched it must be to go from sick to sick.

Now I'll try to get off to sleep and be sure not to worry over H. & T. It is enough for me that you are getting the stray giggle out of them.

I got two Valentines. The two little ward boys each brought me one. Such funny little chaps they are. They'd do anything to come in and get a little chat with me. And Small's Valentine which I daresay you wrote and read. Eye often your shortest notes contain the most.

Goodnight my dear.

Always and lovingly
Emily

P.S. I am so glad Lawren's lectures seem to have been a huge success. Friends of mine wrote and told me full houses and frightfully interested. Yes, we had a lovely visit and Lady Bess was very nice to me, too. They were *both delighted* with Woo's portrait and forbade me to sell it. Lawren wrote a "Not For Sale" tag on its back. I like to have Woo while I live but I have no one to leave her to! Small sends a big hug and is so glad that snowdrops and crocuses are blooming. But Emily still fears your silence means "Emily" is dead. You surely have smothered her in blue snowdrops. I sent a bag full of sundrops to that woman who sent me the cure pills "by air." I hope she gets them alive.

E and S

N.B. Night nurse would not but hoist me awake pulsing me.

Drawing of herself by Emily Carr, 1901. B.C. Archives pdp06119

BIBLIOGRAPHY

Blanchard, Paula. *The Life of Emily Carr.* Vancouver/Toronto: Douglas & McIntyre; Seattle: University of Washington Press, 1987.

Carr, Emily. *The Book of Small.* Toronto: Oxford University Press, 1942. Reprint, Clarke Irwin, 1951.

———. *Fresh Seeing: Two Addresses by Emily Carr.* Toronto: Clarke, Irwin, 1972.

———. *Growing Pains: The Autobiography of Emily Carr.* Toronto: Oxford University Press, 1946. Reprint, Toronto: Clarke, Irwin, 1966.

———. *The Heart of a Peacock.* Toronto: Oxford University Press, 1953.

———. *The House of All Sorts.* Toronto: Oxford University Press, 1944. Reprint, Toronto: Clarke, Irwin, 1967.

———. *Hundreds and Thousands: The Journals of Emily Carr.* Toronto: Clarke, Irwin, 1966.

————. *Klee Wyck*. Toronto: Oxford University Press, 1941.
Revised, Toronto: Clarke, Irwin, 1951.

————. *Pause: A Sketch Book*. Toronto: Clarke, Irwin, 1953.

Crean, Susan. *The Laughing One: A Journey to Emily Carr*. Toronto:
HarperFlamingo, 2001.

Hembroff-Schleicher, Edythe. *Emily Carr: The Untold Story*.
Saanichton, B.C.: Hancock House, 1978.

Tippett, Maria. *Emily Carr: A Biography*. Toronto: Oxford
University Press, 1979. Reprint, Toronto: Penguin,
1982. Reprint, Toronto: Stoddart, 1994.

EMILY CARR: A BRIEF CHRONOLOGY

1863   Richard and Emily Saunders Carr and family emigrate to Victoria, British Columbia.

1871   British Columbia joins Confederation. Emily Carr is born in Victoria on December 12. She has four older sisters: Edith (Dede), Clara, Elizabeth (Lizzie) and Alice.

1875   A brother, Richard (Dick) Henry, is born.

1886   Emily Saunders Carr dies of tuberculosis. Emily is fourteen at the time.

1888   Richard Carr dies. The eldest, Edith, is left in charge of the four children still living at home. Emily is sixteen.

1890/91 Enrols in the California School of Design in San Francisco.

1893   Returns to Victoria, her studies incomplete. Spends the next five years giving art classes to children while continuing to paint and to show her work.

1899   Accompanies her sister Lizzie on a visit to the Presbyterian mission at Ucluelet in April. Meets William (Mayo) Paddon on board the steamship that takes her there. In August she leaves for England. Her brother Richard dies.

1900   Paddon visits Carr in London and proposes marriage; she rejects his suit. After some months, she leaves the Westminster School of Art to study with Julius Olsen and Algernon Talmage at St. Ives in Cornwall, and then with watercolourist John Whiteley in Bushey, Hertfordshire.

1903   Enters the East Anglia Sanatorium where she is diagnosed with hysteria.

1904   After a fifteen-month stay, Carr is released and returns home to Victoria.

1906   Moves to Vancouver where she rents a studio on Granville Street and begins teaching art. Forms a friendship with Sophie Frank, a basket-maker who lives across Burrard Inlet at Squamish Mission.

1907   Travels with her sister Alice to Alaska, where she sees large-scale carvings by indigenous peoples for the first time and conceives the idea of documenting what she perceives as the Natives' disappearing heritage.

1908   Becomes a charter member of the British Columbia Society of Fine Arts and exhibits regularly with them for the next few years. Travels to Kwakwaka'wakw villages at Alert Bay and Campbell River, sketches at nearby Native communities at Sechelt and North Vancouver.

1910   Holds a studio show and auctions her work to raise funds for her sojourn in France. Carr and her sister Alice leave in July for Europe.

1911   Studies with Harry Gibb just east of Paris at Crécy-en-brie and at St. Efflam in Brittany, then at Concarneau with New Zealander Frances Hodgkins.

1912   Resumes her career in Vancouver holding studio exhibitions of her French work.

1913   Holds solo exhibition in Vancouver of some two hundred works on Native themes and delivers "Lecture on Totems." Returns to Victoria and builds a small apartment house called Hill House on Simcoe Street.

1914   The apartment project is a financial failure and Carr spends the next fifteen years trying a variety of ways to make ends meet: raising sheepdogs, selling fruit, making pottery and hooked rugs decorated with Native designs for the tourist trade.

1924   Slowly resumes artistic activities, showing in Seattle and making contact with several American artists including Mark Tobey. She enrols in a correspondence course in fiction writing.

1927   The exhibition *Canadian West Coast Art—Native and Modern*, organized by Marius Barbeau, opens at the National Gallery of Canada. She travels east to Ottawa for the opening, meets the Group of Seven in Toronto and becomes friends with Lawren Harris.

1928   Makes a second major expedition to Native communities up the coast, visiting and sketching at Alert Bay, along the Nass and Skeena Skeena Rivers, and at Queen Charlotte Islands (Haida Gwaii). American artist Mark Tobey gives a class in Carr's studio.

1930   Visits Toronto, Ottawa and New York, where she meets Georgia O'Keeffe. In mid-August makes sketching trips to Native villages around Quatsino Sound on the west coast of Vancouver Island and Port Renfrew.

1933   In the autumn, travels east for the last time to the Chicago World's Fair. Misses the art exhibit but sees work by William Blake at the Art Institute, goes on to Toronto to visit with the Harrises and Houssers. Purchases a trailer, dubbed the Elephant, which serves as a mobile cabin for four summers.

1936   Gives up Hill House and moves to Beckley Street.

1937   Suffers an angina attack and turns to writing when doctors restrict her painting activities.

1938   First annual solo exhibition at the Vancouver Art Gallery.

1939   Suffers a serious heart attack. Ruth Humphrey introduces Carr's writing to Ira Dilworth, who agrees to edit her stories for publication. Sophie Frank dies.

1940   Carr moves in with her sister Alice at 218 St. Andrew's Street, right behind the old family home.

1941   *Klee Wyck* is published and wins the Governor General's Award for Non-fiction.

1942   *The Book of Small* is published. Goes on her last sketching trip.

1943   Major exhibition at the Art Gallery of Toronto.

1944   *House of All Sorts* is published.

1945   Dies on March 2 in Victoria.

ACKNOWLEDGEMENTS

I would like to thank the staff at the British Columbia Archives who provided unstinting support through this complex project. Most particularly, I am grateful for the assistance of Kathryn Bridge, who provided not only access to the original documents but sage advice throughout. I am indebted to Gerta Moray for sharing her insights and her interpretation of the 1913 "Lecture on Totems." And to Saeko Usukawa, I owe the initial impetus.

S.M.C.